I0892182

ECHOES ACROSS THE SEA

Fujian, Persia, and the Arab World

www.royalcollins.com

ILLUSTRATED FUJIAN AND THE MARITIME SILK ROAD

ECHOES ACROSS THE SEA

Fujian, Persia, and the Arab World

Ding Yuling & Lin Han

Edited by Xie Bizhen

Books Beyond Boundaries

ROYAL COLLINS

Echoes across the Sea:
Fujian, Persia, and the Arab World

Ding Yuling & Lin Han
Edited by Xie Bizhen

Translated by Daniel McRyan

First published in 2023 by Royal Collins Publishing Group Inc.
Groupe Publication Royal Collins Inc.
BKM Royalcollins Publishers Private Limited

Headquarters: 550-555 boul. René-Lévesque O Montréal (Québec) H2Z1B1 Canada
India office: 805 Hemkunt House, 8th Floor, Rajendra Place, New Delhi 110 008

Original Edition © Fujian Education Press Co., Ltd.

All rights reserved. Without limiting the rights under copyright reserved above, no part of this publication may be reproduced, stored in or introduced into a retrieval system, or transmitted in any form or by any means (electronic, mechanical, photocopying, recording or otherwise), without the prior written permission of both the copyright owner and the above publisher of this book.

ISBN: 978-1-4878-1124-2

To find out more about our publications, please visit www.royalcollins.com.

Foreword

As early as the 1st century BC, China had established an entire sea route from Xuwen and Hepu of Guangdong Province in southeastern China to the east coast of India; however, the early Chinese navigation was rarely related to the country's economic development. Emperors launched navigations to seek either the elixir of immortality or overseas treasures to maintain the luxurious and decadent lifestyle in the palace. The real overseas trade of China commenced when the Bureau of Foreign Shipping was set up in the Tang Dynasty. It was not until then that overseas trade was included in the national fiscal revenue.

Thanks to its superior geographical condition, Fujian is destined to play a significant role in the history of the overseas transportation and trade of China.

When the Maritime Silk Road is mentioned today, the descriptions tend to paint an easy and poetic picture. However, the formation of the Maritime Silk Road in history has gone through years of thick and thin. The merciless sea had devoured countless lives before the winding Maritime Silk Road came into being. As we look back on its development, we must not forget those great pioneers, namely, the monks who crossed the sea, the common people who went to sea to scrape out a living, the soldiers who went to war abroad, the envoys who were sent overseas, the courtiers who took refuge in foreign countries, the survivors of the shipwrecks, and the crew of Zheng He, who led seven voyages to the West.

It was commonly believed that Fujian ships were the best of all in the Song Dynasty. It was because Fujian had the most advanced navigation and shipbuilding technology of the time that the Quanzhou port had tremendous prosperity. The compass was widely used in navigation and nautical astronomy was developed. The stars were the guide and the wind the fuel. Navigation guidebooks were written and maps were drawn and passed down for generations. The advanced Western technology was also widely adopted in the navigation of Fujian sailors, such as the hourglass and the telescope. Their concept of navigation was evolving rapidly. The saying that "the sea is where Fujian people farm" pinpoints that they sailed for economic benefits. And the leverage of the economy drove them to open the age of Chinese exploration, where voyages were made all over the world and goods shipped overseas.

As per the existing historical data, the footprints of Fujian maritime merchants have been found in Japan and the Korean Peninsula, Southeast Asia, South Asian countries and the African continent. Business people from foreign countries also took Fujian ports as their footholds of trade. Historical documents have recorded that foreign merchant vessels trading with Fujian came from Asia, Africa, Europe, and America. The ancient Maritime Silk Road of China was a joint construction by the people of all countries in the world.

We admire the perfection of the ancient Maritime Silk Road, scrutinize the history of the navigation of Fujian sailors, and respect the outstanding contribution of Fujian ancestors to China's navigation. Their extraordinary sailing activities have left us abundant treasure, such as the sunken ships in the deep ocean, the traded goods that were found everywhere, the harbors silent for many years, the vaguely recognizable buoys, the long navigation picture scrolls, the yellowing nautical guide manuals, and the Mazu temples. The compilation of the illustrated series *Fujian and the Maritime Silk Road* aims to gather these scattered historical fragments piece by piece, so that a full picture of the historical record of Fujian on the ancient Maritime Silk Road can be seen.

The history of the development of the ancient Maritime Silk Road has pinpointed that the Maritime Silk Road came into being thanks to both Chinese and the people of various countries and regions along the way. Now, China's proposal to jointly build the Maritime Silk Road of the 21st Century conforms to the trend of world multi-polarization, economic globalization, and social informatization. Conducive to promoting the orderly and free flow of economic elements, it conforms to the fundamental interests of both China and the international community, highlights the common ideal and pursuit of the human society, and will inject positive energy to the world development.

Reviewing the history of Fujian and the Maritime Silk Road enables us to understand that in the process of building the Maritime Silk Road of the 21st Century, China should make an effort to enhance its comprehensive national strength, develop a value system attractive to all countries, create real soft power, and build its international image and prestige, so as to gradually become a strong global influence.

We shall learn from the history of Fujian on the Maritime Silk Road, explore the secret of success, seize the opportunity, stride into a new era with confidence, and create a victorious future.

Xie Bizhen

Introduction

The vast land of Persia and the Arab world, including most of West Asia and North Africa today, gave birth to the Egyptian, Babylonian, Assyrian, Persian, and Arab civilizations. There, the well-known Persian Empire and Arab Empire were built. Their long coastlines extended to the Atlantic Ocean, the Mediterranean Sea, the Gulf of Oman, the Gulf of Aden, the Red Sea, the Arabian Sea, the Persian Gulf, and the Indian Ocean. Located in the communication hub between the East and West, they have become a trade hub connecting Europe, Asia, and Africa, playing an important role on the world stage.

Judging from documents handed down from ancient times, relics, and inscriptions unearthed during archaeological explorations, Fujian started to communicate with Persia and the Arab world as early as the Tang Dynasty. As overseas trade thrived, the busy collection and distribution of commodities in the coastal ports of Fujian, the strong ships with excellent wind resistance, good stability, agile operation, and safe and reliable ocean-going navigation technology enabled Fujian, Persia, and the Arab world to conduct more frequent exchanges.

Contents

CHAPTER 1

Fujian, Persia, and the Arab World on the Maritime Silk Road

As early as the Western Han Dynasty, Gan Ying reached the Persian Gulf along the Silk Road. The early exchanges between China and Persia and the Arab world started by land, but the massive trade between them was achieved by sea. Because of its geographical environment and social convention, Fujian became an important area for personnel, economic, and trade exchanges with Persia and the Arab world.

1 Fujian's Maritime Tradition

Fujian's temporal and spatial positioning on the sea is not only a remote historical memory but also an accurate portrayal of Fujian's geographical pattern of "eight mountains, one river, and one field" that forced Fujianese to make a living in the sea. The ancient Yue people living on the southeastern coast of China hunted and fished for a living, and they excelled at sailing in rivers and the sea. Fujian's dense river network and long tortuous coastline enabled them to master shipbuilding and navigation very early.

The Western Han canoes unearthed in Shantang Village, Pukou Town, Lianjiang County, Fujian Province in 1975, and the two boat coffins discovered in the Guanyin Cliff Cave in Wuyi Mountain in 1973 and the White Cliff Cave in Wuyi Mountain in 1978 are witnesses to the shipbuilding technology of Yue people. The living environment of these ancestors in the mountains and rivers directly affected their burial system.

Western Han canoe, unearthed in Shantang Village, Pukou Town, Lianjiang County

⦿ A boat coffin on the cliff of Wuyi Mountain

⦿ A boat coffin of Wuyi Mountain

According to the *Records of the Grand Historian*, in 112 BC, the Yue people already possessed certain navigational abilities. Also, *The Book of Yue* and *The Book of Han: Biography of Yan Zhu* vividly depict the lifestyles of the Yue ancestors in the jungles and valleys, who were adept at climbing mountains and sailing the rivers.

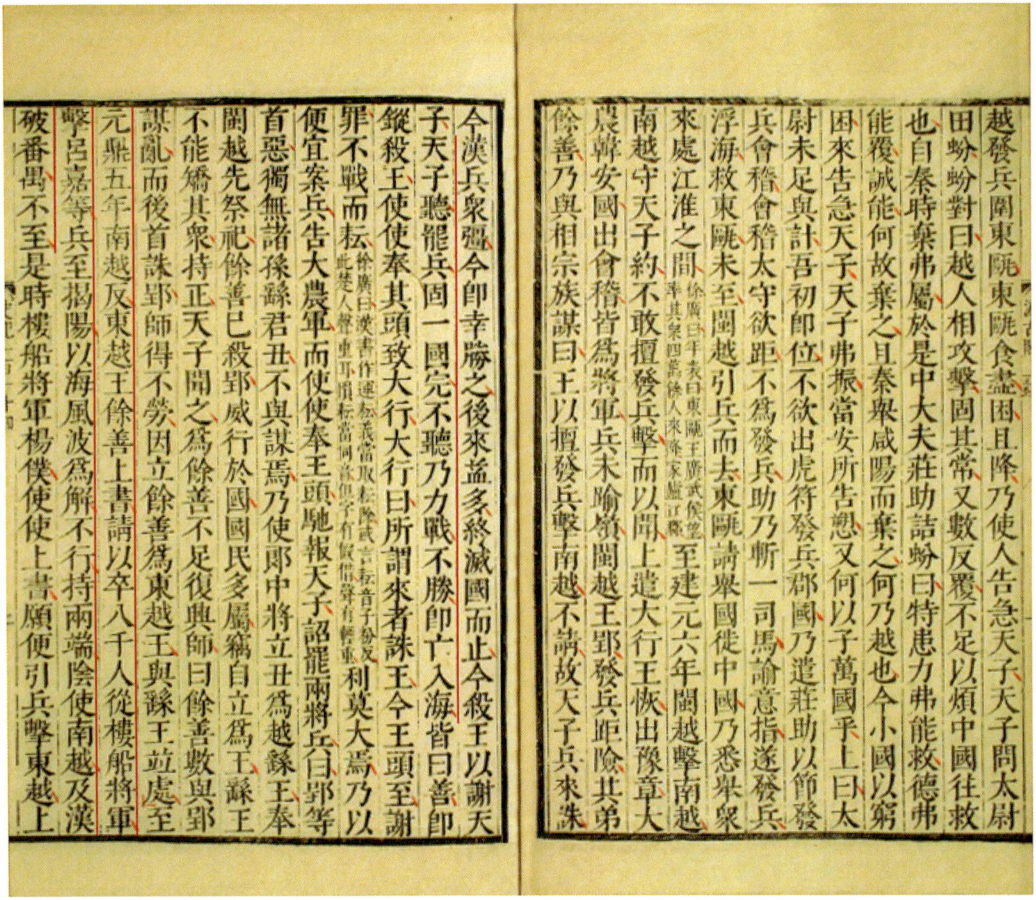

越發兵圍東甌東甌食盡困且降乃使人告急天子天子問太尉田蚡蚡對曰越人相攻擊固其常又數反覆不足以煩中國往救也自秦時棄弗屬於是中大夫莊助詰蚡曰特患力弗能救德弗能覆誠能何故棄之且秦舉咸陽而棄之何乃越也今小國以窮困來告急天子天子弗振當安所告愬又何以子萬國乎上曰太尉未足與計吾初即位不欲出虎符發兵郡國乃遣莊助以節發兵會稽會稽太守欲距不為發兵助乃斬一司馬諭意指遂發兵浮海救東甌未至閩越引兵而去東甌請舉國徙中國乃悉舉衆來處江淮之間（徐廣曰年表云東甌王廣武侯望率其衆四萬餘人來降家廬江郡）至建元六年閩越擊南越南越守天子約不敢擅發兵擊而以聞上遣大行王恢出豫章大農韓安國出會稽皆為將軍兵未踰嶺閩越王郢發兵距險其弟餘善乃與相宗族謀曰王以擅發兵擊南越不請故天子兵來誅今漢兵衆彊今即幸勝之後來益多終滅國而止今殺王以謝天子天子聽罷兵固一國完不聽乃力戰不勝即亡入海皆曰善即鏦殺王使使奉其頭致大行大行曰所為來者誅王今王頭至謝罪不戰而耘（徐廣曰漢書作隕義當取耘除言耘音于紛反此楚人聲重耳隕耘當同義但字有假借聲有輕重）利莫大焉乃以便宜案兵告大農軍而使使奉王頭馳報天子詔罷兩將兵曰郢等首惡獨無諸孫繇君丑不與謀焉乃使郎中將立丑為越繇王奉閩越先祭祀餘善已殺郢威行於國國民多屬竊自立為王繇王不能矯其衆持正天子聞之為餘善不足復興師曰餘善數與郢謀亂而後首誅郢師得不勞因立餘善為東越王與繇王並處至元鼎五年南越反東越王餘善上書請以卒八千人從樓船將軍擊呂嘉等兵至揭陽以海風波為解不行持兩端陰使南越及漢破番禺不至是時樓船將軍楊僕使使上書願便引兵擊東越上

◉ *Records of the Grand Historian: Ranked Biography of Eastern Yue*

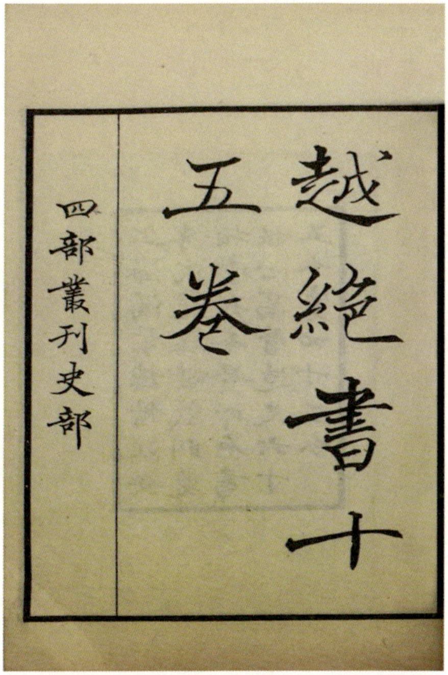

⊙ (LEFT) *Book of Yue*, sample page

⊙ (BELOW) *Book of Han: Biography of Yan Zhu*, sample page

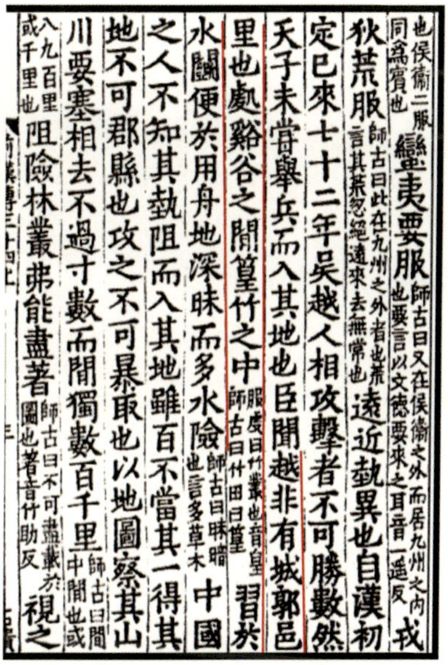

也侯衛二服同爲賓也蠻夷要服師古曰又在侯衛之外而居九州之內也要言以文德要來之耳音一遙反戎狄荒服師古曰此在九州之外者也荒言其荒忽絕遠來去無常也遠近埶異也自漢初定已來七十二年吳越人相攻擊者不可勝數然天子未嘗舉兵而入其地也臣聞越非有城郭邑里也處谿谷之間篁竹之中服虔曰竹叢也音皇師古曰竹田曰篁習於水鬬便於用舟地深昧而多水險師古曰昧暗也言多草木中國之人不知其埶阻而入其地雖百不當其一得其地不可郡縣也攻之不可暴取也以地圖察其山川要塞相去不過寸數而間獨數百千里師古曰間中間也或入九百里或千里也阻險林叢弗能盡著師古曰不可盡載於圖也著音竹助反視之

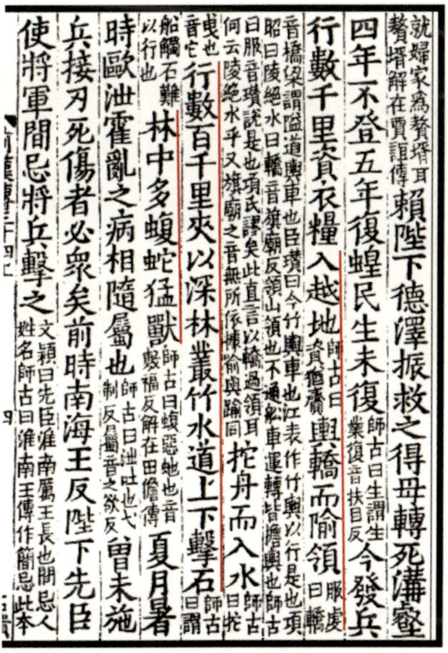

就婦家爲贅壻耳贅壻解在賈誼傳賴陛下德澤振救之得毋轉死溝壑四年不登五年復蝗民生未復師古曰生謂生業復音扶目反今發兵行數千里資衣糧入越地師古曰資猶齎輿轎而隃領服虔曰轎音橋梁謂隘道輿車也臣瓚曰今竹輿車也江表作竹輿以行是也項昭曰陵絕水曰轎音旗廟反領山領也不通船車運轉皆擔輿也師古曰服音瓚說是也項氏謬矣此直言以轎過領耳何云陵絕水乎又旗廟之音無所依據隃與踰同拕舟而入水師古曰拕曳也音它行數百千里夾以深林叢竹水道上下擊石師古曰謂船觸石難以行也林中多蝮蛇猛獸師古曰蝮惡虵也音蝮福反解在田儋傳夏月暑時歐泄霍亂之病相隨屬也師古曰泄吐也弋制反屬音之欲反曾未施兵接刃死傷者必衆矣前時南海王反陛下先臣使將軍間忌將兵擊之文穎曰先臣淮南厲王長也間忌人姓名師古曰淮南王傳作簡忌此本

⦿ The Ancient Ferry of Xinggang

As early as the Three Kingdoms period (AD 220–280), Fuzhou had become one of the critical shipbuilding centers along the coast of China. At the beginning of the 10th century, Wang Shenzhi, the King of Fujian opened Gantang Port in Fuzhou, creating favorable conditions for Fujian's overseas trade to flourish fully. From the Five Dynasties (AD 907–960) to the Northern Song Dynasty (AD 960–1127), Fuzhou had smooth overseas routes, developed overseas trade, and flourished. the poet Su Zhe praised it as the best of the Fujian. After 1472, the imperial court officially identified Fuzhou as the only legal port for exchanges with Ryukyu. Officials and scholars from Ryukyu passed through Fuzhou to Beijing or studied Chinese culture in Fuzhou. Traditional Chinese culture has also radiated through Fuzhou to Japan and Southeast Asia.

Quanzhou, an important port on the ancient Maritime Silk Road, was called Zayton Port in the notes of Western travelers in the Middle Ages. As early as the sixth century, there were already records of Quanzhou's exchanges with Southeast Asian countries. In the Tang Dynasty, it grew into one of the four major ports in China. During the Five Dynasties, Quanzhou was further developed under the governance of Fujian.

With the help of the monsoon winds, the overseas trade routes of Quanzhou Port could reach Northeast Asia, Southeast Asia, South Asia, the Persian Gulf, and the coast of East Africa. In the Song Dynasty, Quanzhou Port conducted trade with 58 overseas countries, including the Philippines and Japan, and in the Yuan Dynasty, the number increased to 98.

The Moon Port of Zhangzhou, located at the estuary of the lower reaches of the Jiulong River, had convenient water and land transportation. Since the implementation of the ban on maritime trade or intercourse with foreign countries in the Ming Dynasty, the Moon Port quietly developed into a base for private overseas trade. In 1567, it was approved by the government to be the only legal port to trade with the East and the West, becoming a metropolis in Southern Fujian, where merchants gathered and foreign ships were moored. The sea route from the Moon Port reached Japan in the east, the Philippines in the south, and Malacca in the west, and was connected with the new route opened by the Europeans, thus forming a complete closed loop of global routes.

⦿ Ruins of the Moon Port of Zhangzhou

2 The Best Ships Were Made in Fujian

As an important carrier of marine culture, ships connect the marine trade networks and build a mobile maritime society with people. To adapt to the vast marine environment, the ancestors of Chinese navigation developed shipbuilding technologies such as the scull, stern rudders, and watertight compartments, which provided safe and reliable support for voyages. And Fujian ships were the best of traditional Chinese ships.

According to archaeological discoveries and literature records, the ships built by the Yue people of Fujian included canoes, *niaochuan* (whose bow resembles a bird's beak), *gechuan*, *louchuan*, arks, and boats. There is evidence of their existence in the *Book of Yue* and *The Huainanzi*.

It took a long time for Chinese ships to develop from simple canoes and bamboo rafts in the early days to complex wooden boats, flat boats, and sharp-built vessels. From the ancient sailing system, old ships can be divided into Fujian ships, Guangzhou ships, and Sha ships. Fujian ships are representative of sharp-built ships.

⊙ *Niaochuan* model

◉ (ABOVE) Fujian ship—Princess Taiping (replica)

◉ (RIGHT) Guangzhou ship—Jinhuaxing (replica)

⦿ Sha ship model

In AD 269, the Eastern Wu government established the *dianchuan xiaowei* (a shipbuilding officer) in Fuzhou to supervise sea shipbuilding. Because of the need for overseas trade, the local shipbuilding industry flourished. In the Song Dynasty, there were special shipbuilding workshops in Fuzhou, Putian, Quanzhou, and Zhangzhou. Both *Quan Nan Ge* by Xie Lü and *Lun Zhou Ji Zhi Li* by Lü Yihao confirm the high status of Fujian ships in sea transportation at the time.

Quan Nan Ge by Xie Lü

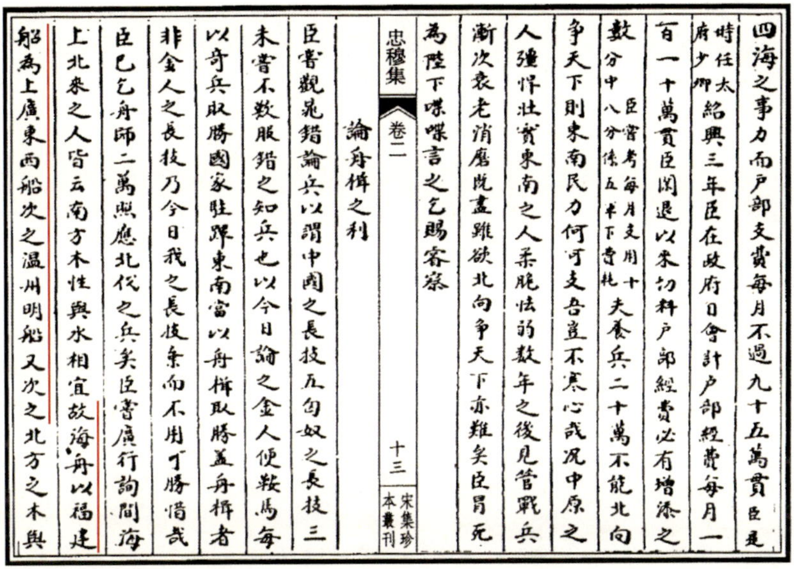

四海之事力而戶部支費每月不過九十五萬貫臣是
時任太府少卿 紹興三年臣在政府日會計戶部經費每月一
百一十萬貫臣閑退以來切料戶部經費必有增添之
數 臣嘗考每月支用十分中八分係五軍下費耗 夫養兵二十萬不能北向
爭天下則東南民力何可支吾豈不寒心哉況中原之
人彊悍壯實東南之人柔脆怯弱數年之後見管戰兵
漸次衰老消磨既盡雖欲北向爭天下亦難矣臣冒死
為陛下喋喋言之乞賜睿察

忠穆集 卷二 十三 宋集珍本叢刊

論舟楫之利

臣嘗觀晁錯論兵以謂中國之長技五匈奴之長技三
未嘗不歎服錯之知兵也以今日論之金人便鞍馬每
以奇兵取勝國家駐蹕東南當以舟楫取勝蓋舟楫者
非金人之長技乃今日我之長技棄而不用可勝惜哉
臣已乞舟師二萬與應北伐之兵矣臣嘗廣行詢問海
上北來之人皆云南方木性與水相宜故海舟以福建
船為上廣東西船次之溫州明船又次之北方之木與

Lun Zhou Ji Zhi Li by Lü Yihao, sample page

The Fujian ship is a collective name for ocean-going wooden ships built along the coast of Fujian. This kind of ship is sturdy, with excellent seaworthiness and seakeeping capacity, as seen in the Song Dynasty seacraft unearthed in Quanzhou Bay. It is characterized by a colossal hull, a sharp hull bottom, a wide surface, a sharp bow, and a square tail. Its bottom has a thick keel, and its cabin is watertight. There is a single-layer or multi-layer ship deck structure, whose caulking is tung putty, and the shipbuilding materials are seawater-resistant wood such as fir, pine, and camphor, wood that is abundant in Fujian.

The ships of Quanzhou Bay in the Song Dynasty adopted the overlapping joint structure of multiple plates, which were nailed together with iron nails in all sorts of shapes, square, round, flat, and so on. Also, various nailing

⊙ Song Dynasty ship displayed in the Quanzhou Bay Ancient Ship Exhibition Hall

techniques were applied to make the ship structures robust and watertight. At that time, some Southeast Asian and South Asian boats were just "sutured" together with a kind of plant fiber, as they didn't know how to use iron nails.

The Travels of Marco Polo also depicted the unique multi-plate structure of Fujian ships in detail. Those ships are the summary of ancient Chinese craftsmen's long-term practice of building wooden sailboats, which had the advanced nature of the times.

⦿ The excavation site of the Song Dynasty ship in Quanzhou Bay in 1974

⦿ The multi-plate structure of the Song Dynasty ship in Quanzhou Bay

⦿ Iron nails of the Song Dynasty ship in Quanzhou Bay

The ancient Song Dynasty ship in Quanzhou Bay is the largest and oldest seacraft discovered in China. At the same time, it is the only ancient seacraft found in China that has returned from abroad and unearthed. Whether in the history of overseas trade or the history of ancient ships, this ship is an essential historical coordinate. In 1984, Joseph Needham, the famous British expert in the history of science, visited this ancient ship in Quanzhou and praised it as one of the most important discoveries in the history of science in China.

⊙ In 1984, Joseph Needham visited the Quanzhou Bay Ancient Ship Exhibition Hall

Watertight compartment technology is a major invention of ancient Chinese shipbuilding technology. It uses watertight partitions to divide the cabin into mutually impermeable compartments. Each watertight compartment is surrounded by a shifting board, shelling plate, underwater plate, and ship deck. The shifting board and the shelling plate are connected via iron hooks, and "ribs" are installed on both sides to support the shelling plate. In addition, as raw materials, ramie, lime, and tung oil are blended in a certain proportion to create caulking, which is filled into the gap between the wooden boards in the cabin to make it watertight. It not only increases the strength of the hull but also improves the water tightness of the ship and facilitates the subdivision management of the cargo. In addition, the partition of the layers of thick shifting boards and tightly nailed shelling plates can support the ship from another angle, making the hull stronger. This hull structure divides the hull into several cabins so that even if the vessel suffers damage in one or two spots during sailing, it will not sink, which improves its safety performance. Except for a small water hole near the keel at the bottom of the cabin, all the bulkheads have the excellent water tightness which is characteristic of these bulkheads.

⊙ The water hole near the baseboard of a Song Dynasty ship in Quanzhou Bay

On the medieval Maritime Silk Road, merchant ships from various countries traveled east and west in the Western Pacific and Indian Oceans. However, in the event of an accident, foreign ships easily sank. Only the Chinese vessels could continue to sail until they reached their destination. Then damage during the accident could be repaired thanks to the application of watertight compartment technology. Chinese ships were installed with this kind of waterproof compartment since the Tang Dynasty, and in the Song Dynasty, its design and application became more common and mature. In 1795, the West adopted this technology for the first time, nearly five hundred years later than China. Today, this technology is still widely used in modern shipbuilding.

In 2008, the Fujian ship watertight compartment manufacturing technique was included in the second batch of the State-Level Non-Material Cultural Heritage List. In 2010, UNESCO included it in *The List of Intangible Cultural Heritage in Need of Urgent Safeguarding*.

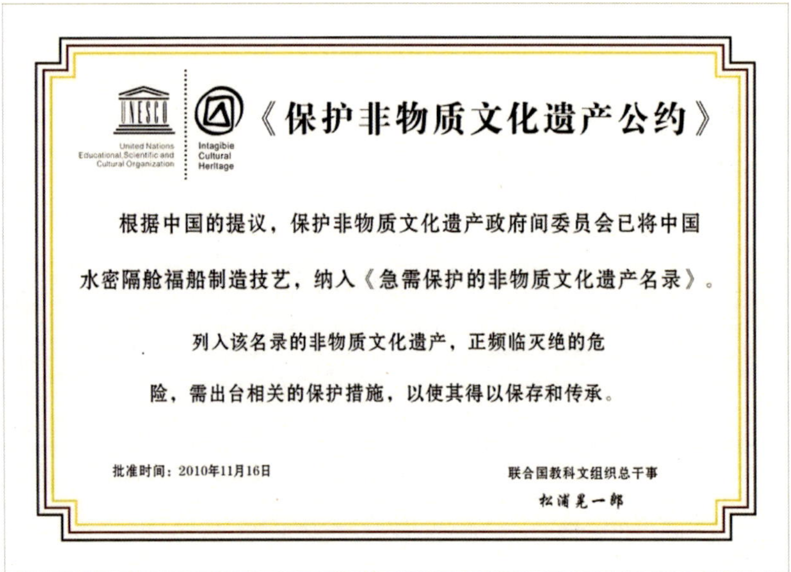

UNESCO
United Nations Educational, Scientific and Cultural Organization
Intagible Cultural Heritage

《保护非物质文化遗产公约》

根据中国的提议，保护非物质文化遗产政府间委员会已将中国水密隔舱福船制造技艺，纳入《急需保护的非物质文化遗产名录》。

列入该名录的非物质文化遗产，正频临灭绝的危险，需出台相关的保护措施，以使其得以保存和传承。

批准时间：2010年11月16日

联合国教科文组织总干事
松浦晃一郎

Certificate of the Fujian ship watertight compartment manufacturing technique in *The List of Intangible Cultural Heritage in Need of Urgent Safeguarding*

In the Yuan Dynasty, the Mongolian army crossed the sea to Japan and went south to ancient Vietnam. The warships that they sailed were primarily built in Fujian. Marco Polo escorted Princess Kököjin to get married in Persia, and the ships in her fleet were built in Citong, Quanzhou.

⊙ Houzhu Port of Quanzhou, Marco Polo departure point

⊙ A model of the Citong ship from the Yuan Dynasty made according to the description in *The Travels of Marco Polo*

In the Ming Dynasty, the title of Fujian ships became official. There are descriptions of Fujian ships in both *Ji Xiao Xin Shu* by Qi Jiguang and *Zheng Qi Tang Ji* by Yu Dayou. The excellent performance of the Fujian ship made it the first choice as the warship for the navy of the Ming and Qing dynasties and the travel ships for overseas missions. It was with Fujian ships that Zheng He made the voyages to the West.

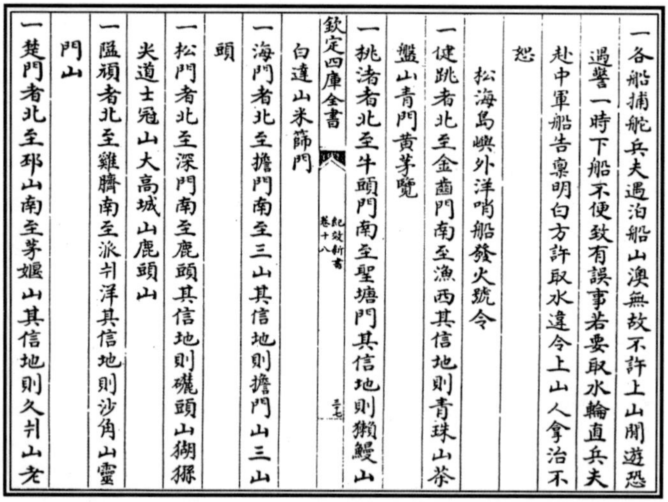

一各船捕舵兵夫遇泊船山澳無故不許上山閒遊恐
遇警一時下船不便致有誤事若要取水輪直兵夫
赴中軍船告稟明白方許取水違令上山人拿治不
恕
松海島嶼外洋哨船發火號令
一健跳者北至金齒門南至漁西其信地則青珠山茶
盤山青門黃茅覽
一桃渚者北至牛頭門南至聖塘門其信地則獺鰻山
欽定四庫全書 紀效新書 卷十八 三十七
白達山米篩門
一海門者北至擔門南至三山其信地則擔門山三山
頭
一松門者北至深門南至鹿頭其信地則礁頭山猢猻
尖道士冠山大高城山鹿頭山
一溫嶺者北至雞籠南至泒引洋其信地則沙角山靈
門山
一楚門者北至邪山南至茅嶼山其信地則久引山老

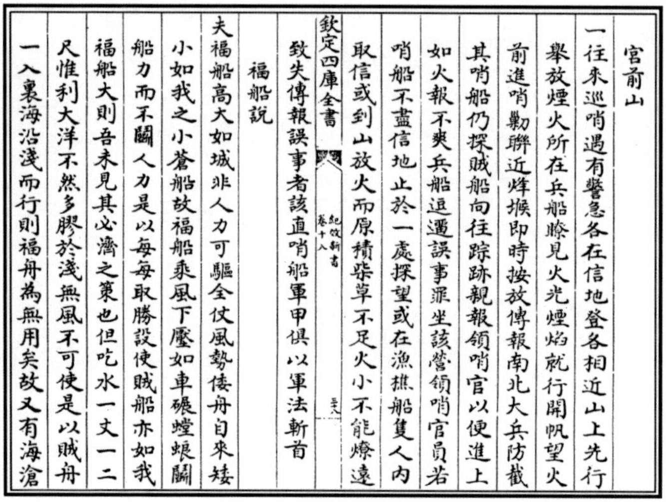

宮前山
一往來巡哨遇有警急各在信地登各相近山上先行
舉放煙火所在兵船瞭見火光煙焰就行開帆望火
前進哨勦聯近烽堠即時按放傳報南北大兵防截
其哨船仍探賊船向往蹤跡親報領哨官以便進上
如火報不爽兵船逗遛誤事罪坐該營領哨官員若
哨船不盡信地止於一處探望或在漁撫船隻人內
取信或到山放火而原積柴草不足火小不能燎遠
欽定四庫全書 紀效新書 卷十八 三十八
致失傳報誤事者該直哨船軍甲俱以軍法斬首
福船說
夫福船高大如城非人力可驅全仗風勢倭舟自來矮
小如我之小蒼船故福船乘風下壓如車碾螳蜋鬬
船力而不鬬人力是以每每取勝設使賊船亦如我
福船大則吾未見其必濟之策也但吃水一丈一二
尺惟利大洋不然多膠於淺無風不可使是以賊舟
一入裏海沿淺而行則福舟為無用矣故又有海滄

Records of Fujian ships in *Ji Xiao Xin Shu* by Qi Jiguang

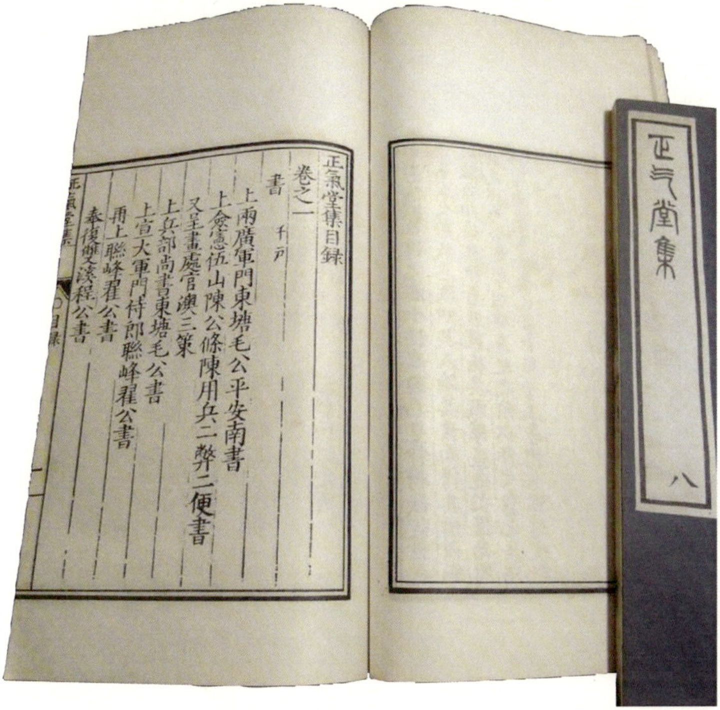

正氣堂集目録
卷之一
書
上兩廣軍門東塘毛公平安南書
上僉憲伍山陳公條陳用兵二弊二便書
又呈書處官澳三策
上兵部尚書東塘毛公書
上宣大軍門侍郎聯峰翟公書
再上聯峰翟公書
奉復雙溪程公書

⊙ *Zheng Qi Tang Ji* by Yu Dayou, sample page

⊙ Model of Zheng He's fleet

In the completed painting from the first half of the 18th century, *Tang Ships*, collected in the Matsuura Museum of Historical Materials in Hirado, Japan, there is significant similarity between the Nanjing ship built in Fuzhou, the Canton ship built in Fuzhou, Xiamen ship, and Taiwan ship. It shows the various forms of Fujian ships.

⊙ Nanjing ship built in Fuzhou

⦿ (ABOVE) Canton ship built in Fuzhou

⦿ (BELOW) Taiwan ship

風切

⦿ Xiamen Ship

Around 2000, traditional wooden sailboat building could still be seen along the coast of Quanzhou. Standard shipbuilding tools in Quanzhou include axes, hoes, planers, chisels, and more. As traditional wooden sailboats have become outdated, a complete set of such tools is now less common.

⦿ Shipbuilding tools: planers

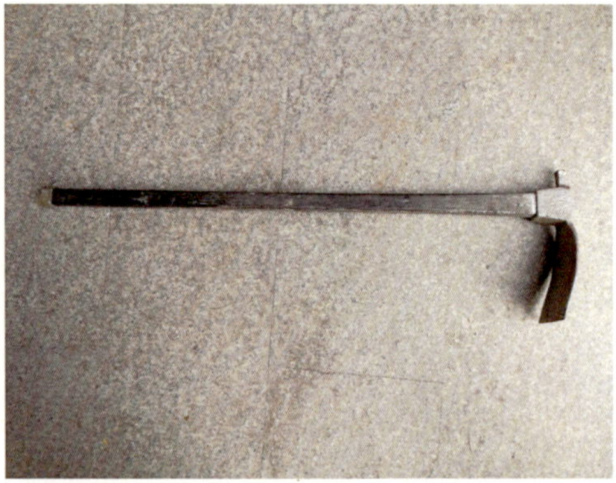

⦿ Hoe ax

⦿ Hammer

⦿ Ax

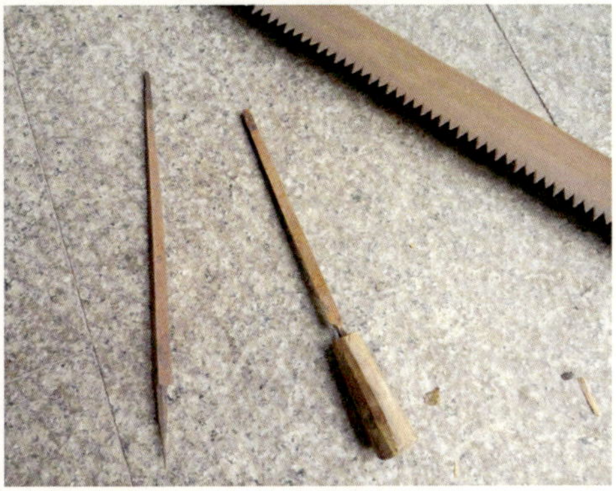

◉ Saw file

◉ Saw

◉ Duct

◉ Rotary drill

◉ Chisel

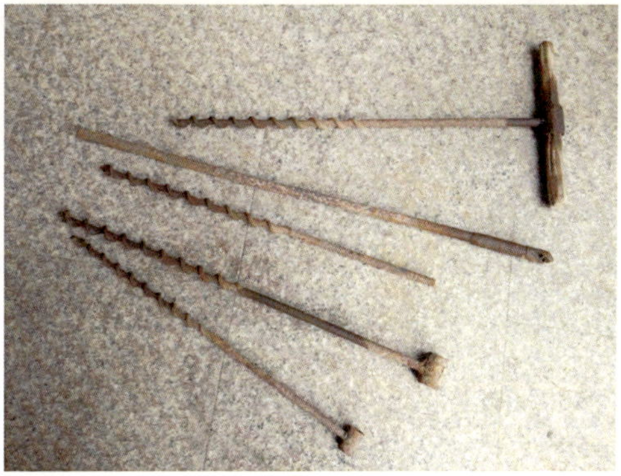

◉ Drill

3 The Routes from Fujian to Persia and the Arab World

Historically, the exchanges between Fujian and Persia and the Arab world started in the Tang Dynasty. Porcelain, silk, tea from China, spices, and jewelry from Southeast Asia, as well as gems and ivory from Africa, were transported to all parts of the world through the Maritime Silk Road, which promoted the exchange of people in different regions and the communication of cultures.

As early as AD 834, a special proclamation was issued to attract businessmen from the Arab Empire to China. *The Book of Min · Linshan* by He Qiaoyuan (1558–1632) even mentions that four disciples of Muhammad preached in China in the middle of the reign of Wude of the Tang Dynasty (618–626).

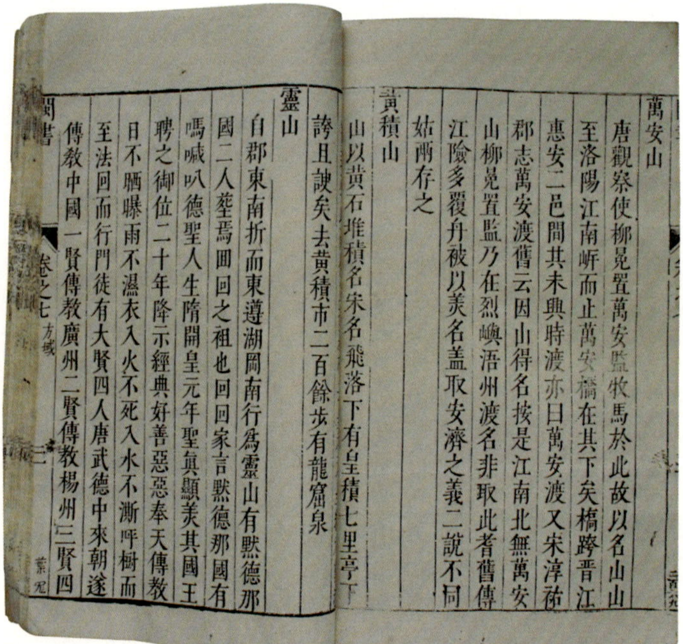
萬安山
唐觀察使柳冕置萬安監牧馬於此故以名山山
至洛陽江南岍而止萬安橋在其下矣橋跨晉江
惠安二邑間其未興時渡亦曰萬安渡又宋淳祐
郡志萬安渡舊云因山得名按是江南北無萬安
山柳冕置監乃在烈嶼浯州渡名非取此者舊傳
江險多覆舟祓以美名蓋取安濟之義二說不同
姑兩存之
黃積山
山以黃石堆積名宋名飛落下有皇積七里亭下
詩且諛矣去黃積市二百餘歩有龍窟泉
靈山
自郡東南折而東遵湖岡南行為靈山有默德那
國二人葬焉回回之祖也回回家言默德那國有
嗎喊叭德聖人生隋開皇元年聖真顯美其國王
聘之御位二十年降示經典好善惡惡奉天傳教
日不晒暴雨不濡衣入火不死入水不溺呼樹而
至法回而行門徒有大賢四人唐武德中來朝遂
傳教中國一賢傳教廣州二賢傳教楊州三賢四

⊙ *Book of Min · Linshan* (1)

Under the governance of the Wangs, the Min Kingdom implemented the national policy of attracting overseas merchants. Wang Shenzhi opened up Gantang Port, making Fuzhou increasingly prosperous in overseas trade. Quanzhou has also opened the Quanzhou era by promoting overseas trade policies.

⦿ Portrait of Wang Shenzhi

⦿ Temple of Three Min Kings in Quanzhou

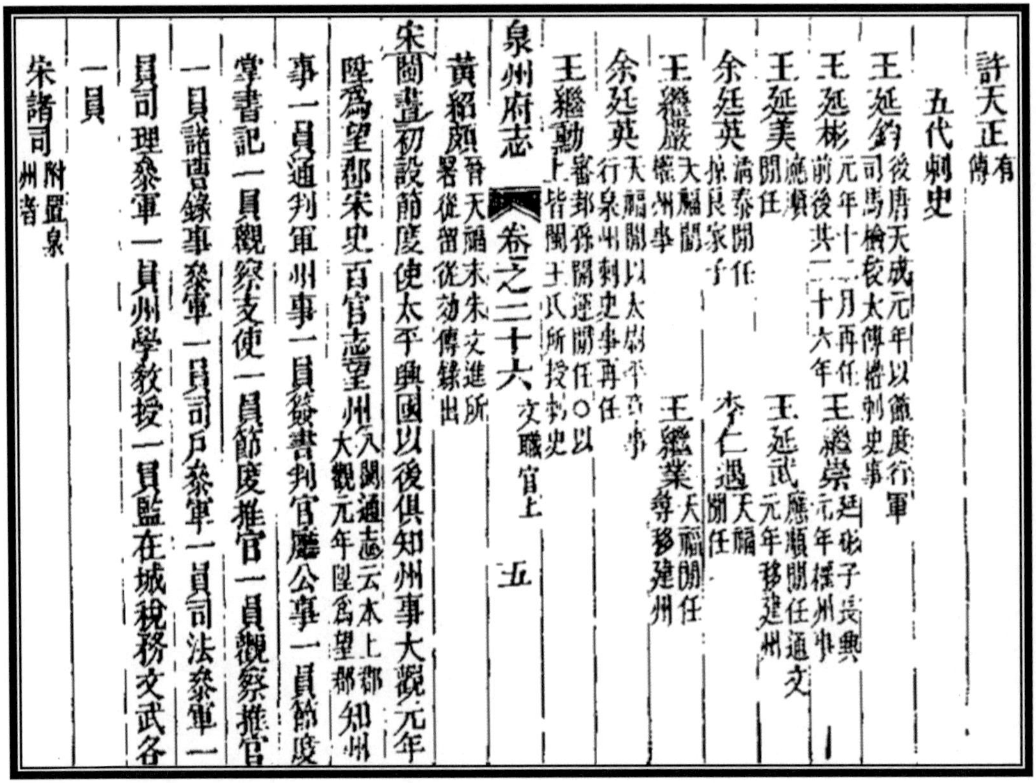

許天正有傳
五代刺史
王延鈞後唐天成元年以節度行軍司馬檢校太傅攝刺史事
王延彬元年十二月再任前後共二十六年 王繼崇延彬子長興元年權州事
王延美應順開任 王延武應順元年移建州任通文
余廷英清泰開任 李仁遇天福開任
余廷英掠良家子
王繼嚴天福開權州事 王繼業天福開任尋移建州
余廷英天福開以太尉平章事行泉州刺史事再任
王繼勳審知孫開運開任○以上皆閩王氏所授刺史
泉州府志 卷之二十六 文職官上 五
黃紹頗晉天福末朱文進所署從留從效傳錄出
宋閩置初設節度使太平興國以後俱知州事大觀元年陞為望郡宋史百官志望州入閩通志云本上郡大觀元年陞為望郡知州
事一員通判軍州事一員簽書判官廳公事一員節度
掌書記一員觀察支使一員節度推官一員觀察推官
一員諸曹錄事參軍一員司戶參軍一員司法參軍一
員司理參軍一員州學教授一員監在城稅務文武各
一員
宋諸司附置泉州者

⦿ A list of the Wangs as prefectural governors in Quanzhou recorded in *Quanzhou Prefecture Chronicles* during the reign of Emperor Qianlong of the Qing Dynasty

Due to the improvement of the economic status of the port city and the convenience of transactions, Quanzhou became the economic center of the Min Kingdom during Five Dynasties and Ten Kingdoms period (AD 909–949) and was designated as a coinage base. In the Chengtian Temple of Quanzhou, the coinage site of the Min period was discovered, and a large number of Yonglong Tongbao were unearthed. These are also the only coin models of the Five Dynasties and Ten Kingdoms period found in China so far, filling in a blank space in the history of Chinese coinage.

⦿ The archaeological site of the coin model of Yonglong Tongbao in the Five Dynasties

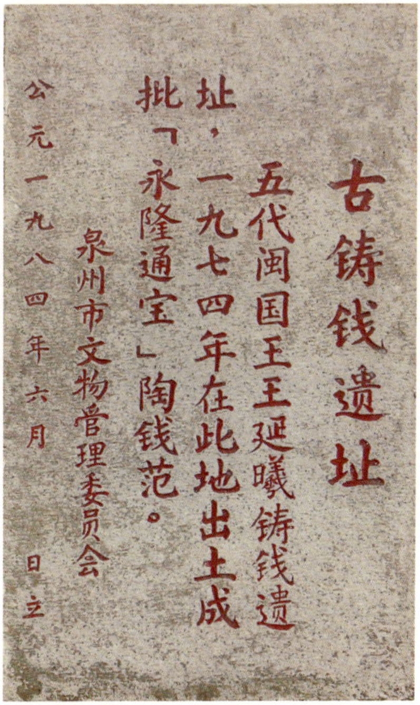

⦿ (ABOVE) The coin model of Yonglong Tongbao unearthed at the Chengtian Temple of Quanzhou

⦿ (RIGHT) The ancient coin-casting site monument in Chengtian Temple

In February 1965, three malachite green-glazed vases unearthed from Liu Hua's tomb in Fuzhou originated in ancient Persia. Its shape and decoration have a unique style from West Asia and Central Asia, which was introduced through the Maritime Silk Road. It is a physical witness to Fujian and Persia maritime trade in the Middle Ages.

⦿ Persian malachite green-glazed vase unearthed from Liu Hua's tomb

Since the Song Dynasty, as the national economic center moved to the south, the maritime trade in Fujian also ushered in a glorious period. In particular, the southward relocation of the Song capital and the Quanzhou Bureau for Foreign Shipping establishment significantly promoted Quanzhou's overseas trade. During this period, it became a tremendous eastern port with trade relations with nearly 100 countries and regions. During this period, maritime merchants also opened up many sea trade routes from Quanzhou to foreign neighbors, recorded in *Meng Liang Lu* by Wu Zimu of the Southern Song Dynasty.

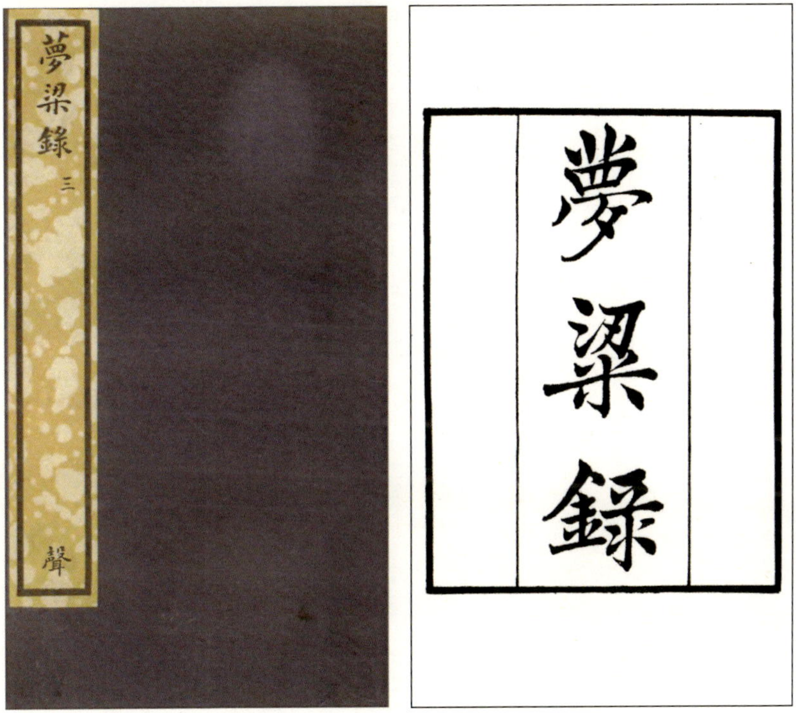

⊙ *Meng Liang Lu*, sample page

Zhao Rushi (1170–1231), a citizen of the Southern Song Dynasty, recorded in his *A Description of Barbarian Nations, Records of Foreign People,* many routes from Quanzhou to countries in the Southeast, Western, and Eastern Oceans. The routes to the Arabian Peninsula and Africa are as follows.

The route from Quanzhou to Lambri of India, Kollam, and the Arabian Peninsula: depart from Quanzhou Port, pass Srivijaya, cross the Strait of Malacca, sail along the coast of Bangladesh, and reach Kollam. It takes around 40 days to get to Lambri. After winter, only when the south wind blows can the ships cross the Indian Ocean and enter the Persian Gulf to reach Persia and Arabia.

The route from Quanzhou to the Gulf of Aden and East Africa's Barbary Coast (Somalia of today) and Zanzibar: depart from Quanzhou Port, pass through the South China Sea, Srivijaya, Kollam, and reach the Persian Gulf, and then from the Persian Gulf, sail southwest along the Arabian Coast, and reach the Barbary Coast and Zanzibar. A one-way tailwind trip takes 160 days, and a round trip takes about two years.

In addition, *A Description of Barbarian Nations, Records of Foreign People* also records the geographical conditions and religious customs of the Arab countries at that time, such as the Arab Empire, Mecca, Baghdad, and Basra. The history of relations in the Arab region and the history of the Hui people in Fujian are of great value.

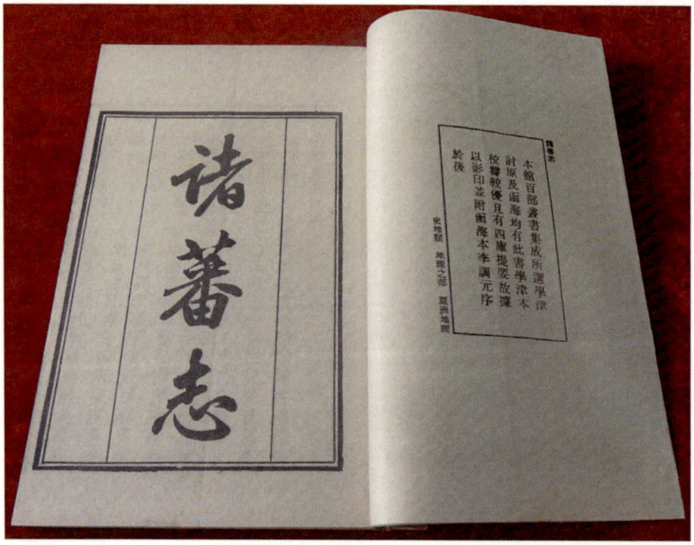

⊙ *A Description of Barbarian Nations, Records of Foreign People*, sample page

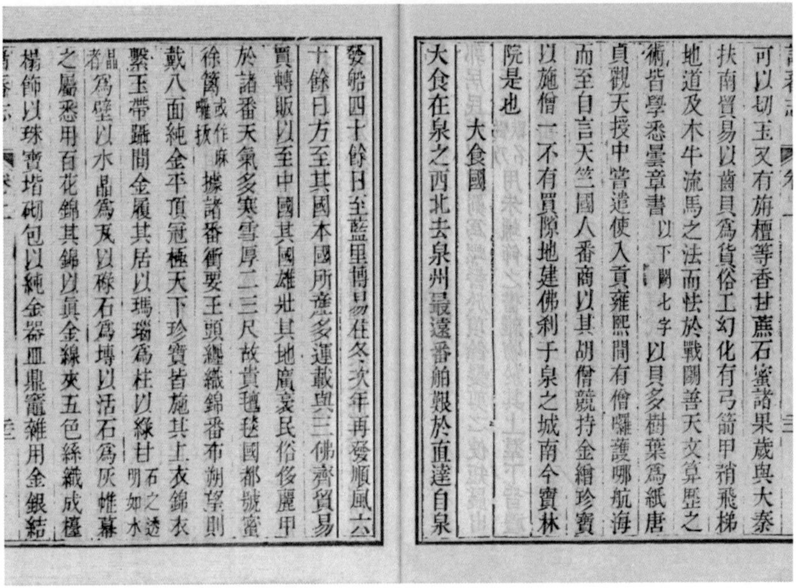

可以切玉又有旃檀等香甘蔗石蜜諸果歲與大秦
扶南貿易以齒貝爲貨俗工幻化有弓箭甲矟飛梯
地道及木牛流馬之法而怯於戰鬬善天文筭歷之
術皆學悉曇章書以下闕七字以貝多樹葉爲紙唐
貞觀天授中嘗遣使入貢雍熙間有僧囉護哪航海
而至自言天竺國人番商以其胡僧競持金繒珍寶
以施僧一不有買隙地建佛刹于泉之城南今寶林
院是也

大食國

大食在泉之西北去泉州最遠番舶艱於直達自泉
發舶四十餘日至藍里博易住冬次年再發順風六
十餘日方至其國本國所產多運載與三佛齊貿易
賈轉販以至中國其國雄壯其地廣袤民俗侈麗甲
於諸番天氣多寒雪厚二三尺故貴氈毯國都號蜜
徐籬或作麻囉拔據諸番衝要王頭纏織錦番布朔望則
戴八面純金平頂冠極天下珍寶皆施其上衣錦衣
繫玉帶躡間金履其居以瑪瑙爲柱以綠甘石之透明如水
晶者爲壁以水晶爲瓦以碌石爲塼以活石爲灰帷幕
之屬悉用百花錦其錦以真金線夾五色絲織成檯
榻飾以珠寶堦砌包以純金器皿鼎竈雜用金銀結

⦿ Records of the Arab Empire in *A Description of Barbarian Nations, Records of Foreign People*

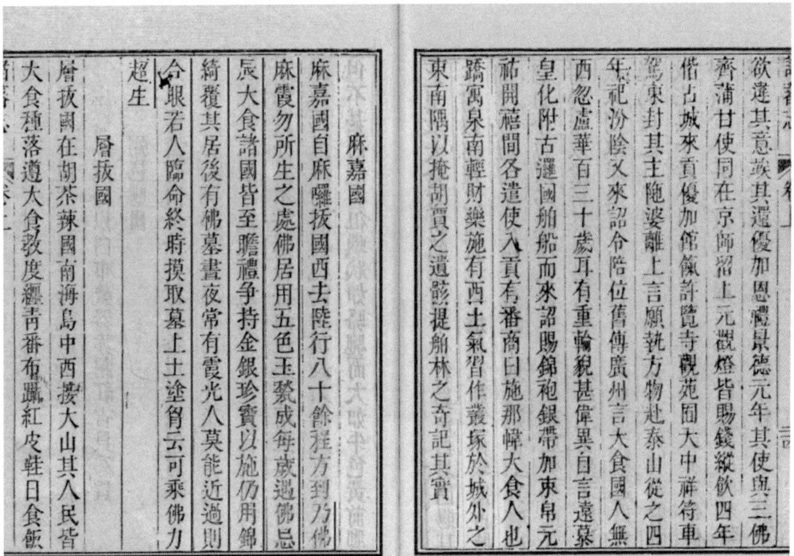

欲逵其意遂其還優加恩禮景德元年其使與三佛
齊蒲甘使同在京師留上元觀燈皆賜錢縱飲四年
偕古城來貢優加館餼許覽寺觀苑囿大中祥符車
駕東封其主陁婆離上言願執方物赴泰山從之四
年祀汾陰又來詔令陪位舊傳廣州言大食國人無
西忽盧華百三十歲耳有重輪貌甚偉異自言遠慕
皇化附古邏國舶船而來詔賜錦袍銀帶加束帛元
祐開禧間各遣使入貢有番商曰施那幃大食人也
蹻寓泉南輕財樂施有西土氣習作叢塚於城外之
東南隅以掩胡賈之遺骸提舶林之奇記其實

麻嘉國

麻嘉國自麻囉拔國西去陸行八十餘程方到乃佛
麻霞勿所生之處佛居用五色玉甃成每歲遇佛忌
辰大食諸國皆至瞻禮爭持金銀珍寶以施仍用錦
綺覆其居後有佛墓晝夜常有霞光人莫能近過則
合眼若人臨命終時摸取墓上土塗胷云可乘佛力
超生

層拔國

層拔國在胡茶辣國南海島中西接大山其人民皆
大食種落遵大食教度纏青番布躡紅皮鞋日食飯

⦿ Records of Mecca in *A Description of Barbarian Nations, Records of Foreign People*

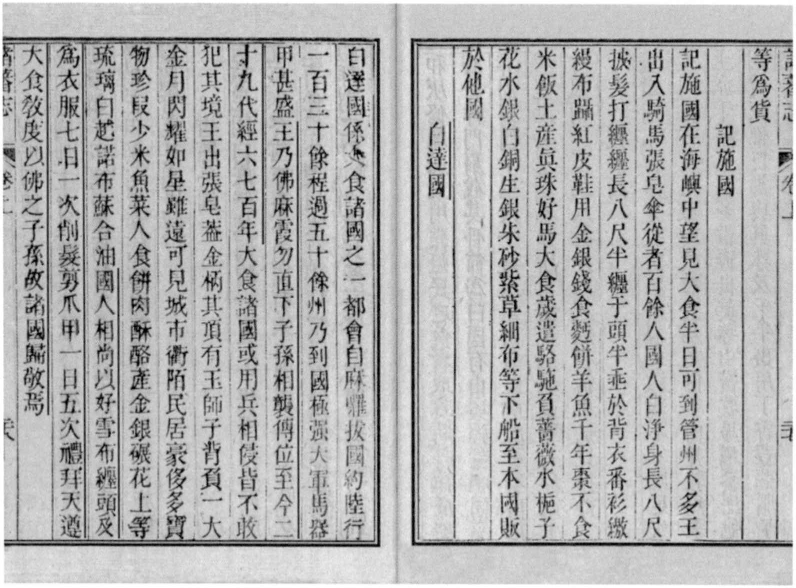

等爲貨
記施國
記施國在海嶼中望見大食半日可到管州不多王
出入騎馬張皂傘從者百餘人國人白淨身長八尺
披髪打纏纏長八尺半纏于頭半垂於背衣番衫繳
緩布躡紅皮鞋用金銀錢食麪餅羊魚千年棗不食
米飯土產眞珠好馬大食歲遣駱駝負薔薇水梔子
花水銀白銅生銀朱砂紫草細布等下船至本國販
於他國
白達國
白達國係大食諸國之一都會自麻囉拔國約陸行
一百三十餘程過五十餘州乃到國極強大軍馬器
甲甚盛王乃佛麻霞勿直下子孫相襲傳位至今二
十九代經六七百年大食諸國或用兵相侵皆不敢
犯其境王出張皂蓋金柄其頂有玉師子背負一大
金月閃耀如星雖遠可見城市衢陌民居豪侈多寶
物珍叚少米魚菜人食餅肉酥酪產金銀碾花上等
琉璃白越諾布蘇合油國人相尚以好雪布纏頭及
爲衣服七日一次削髮剪爪甲一日五次禮拜天遵
大食教度以佛之子孫故諸國歸敬焉

⊙ Records of Baghdad in *A Description of Barbarian Nations, Records of Foreign People*

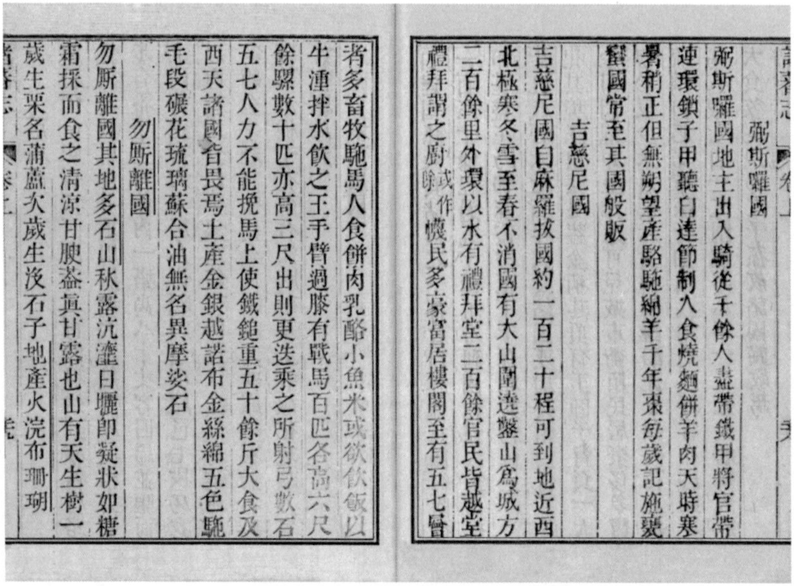

弼斯囉國
弼斯囉國地主出入騎從千餘人盡帶鐵甲將官帶
連環鎖子甲聽白達節制人食燒麪餅羊肉天時寒
暑稍正但無朔望產駱駝綿羊千年棗每歲記施甕
蠻國常至其國般販
吉慈尼國
吉慈尼國自麻羅拔國約一百二十程可到地近西
北極寒冬雪至春不消國有大山圍遶鑿山爲城方
二百餘里外環以水有禮拜堂二百餘官民皆越堂
禮拜謂之廚除或作懷民多豪富居樓閣至有五七層
耆多畜牧馳馬人食餅肉乳酪小魚米或欲飲飯以
牛運拌水飲之王手臂過膝有戰馬百匹各高六尺
餘騾數十匹亦高三尺出則更迭乘之所射弓數石
五七人力不能挽馬上使鐵鎚重五十餘斤大食及
西天諸國皆畏焉土產金銀越諾布金絲綿五色駝
毛段碾花琉璃蘇合油無名異摩娑石
勿斯離國
勿斯離國其地多石山秋露沆瀣日曬即凝狀如糖
霜採而食之清涼甘腴蓋眞甘露也山有天生樹一
歲生栗名蒲蘆次歲生沒石子地產火浣布珊瑚

⊙ Records of Basra in *A Description of Barbarian Nations, Records of Foreign People*

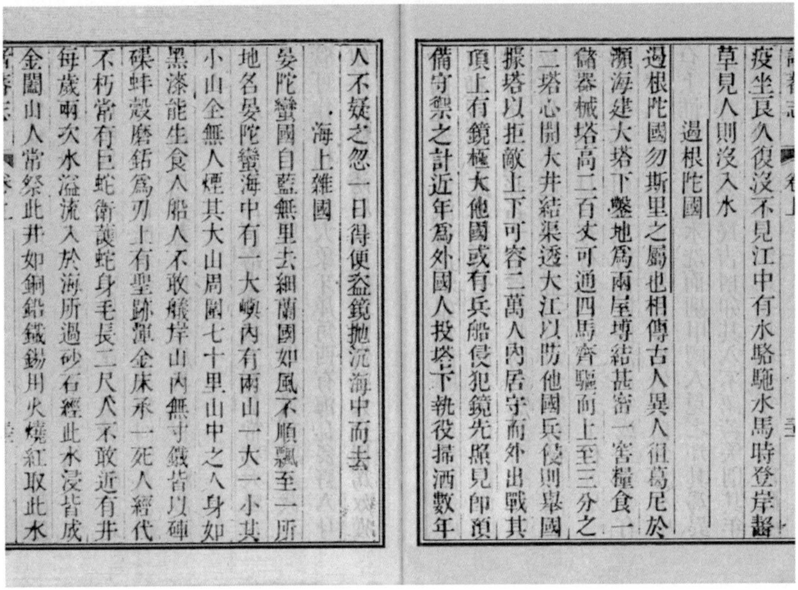

疫坐良久復沒不見江中有水駱駝水馬時登岸齧
草見人則沒入水
遏根陀國
遏根陀國勿斯里之屬也相傳古人異人徂葛尼於
瀕海建大塔下鑿地爲兩屋塼結甚密一窖糧食一
儲器械塔高二百丈可通四馬齊驅而上至三分之
二塔心開大井結渠透大江以防他國兵侵則舉國
據塔以拒敵上下可容二萬人內居守而外出戰其
頂上有鏡極大他國或有兵船侵犯鏡先照見即預
備守禦之計近年爲外國人投塔下執役掃洒數年
人不疑之忽一日得便盜鏡拋沉海中而去
海上雜國
晏陀蠻國自藍無里去細蘭國如風不順飄至一所
地名晏陀蠻海中有一大嶼內有兩山一大一小其
小山全無人煙其大山周圍七十里山中之人身如
黑漆能生食人船人不敢艤岸山內無寸鐵皆以硨
磲蚌殼磨銛爲刃上有聖跡渾金床承一死人經代
不朽常有巨蛇衛護蛇身毛長二尺人不敢近有井
每歲兩次水溢流入於海所過砂石經此水浸皆成
金闔山人常祭此井如銅鉛鐵錫用火燒紅取此水

⦿ Records of Alexandria in *A Description of Barbarian Nations, Records of Foreign People*

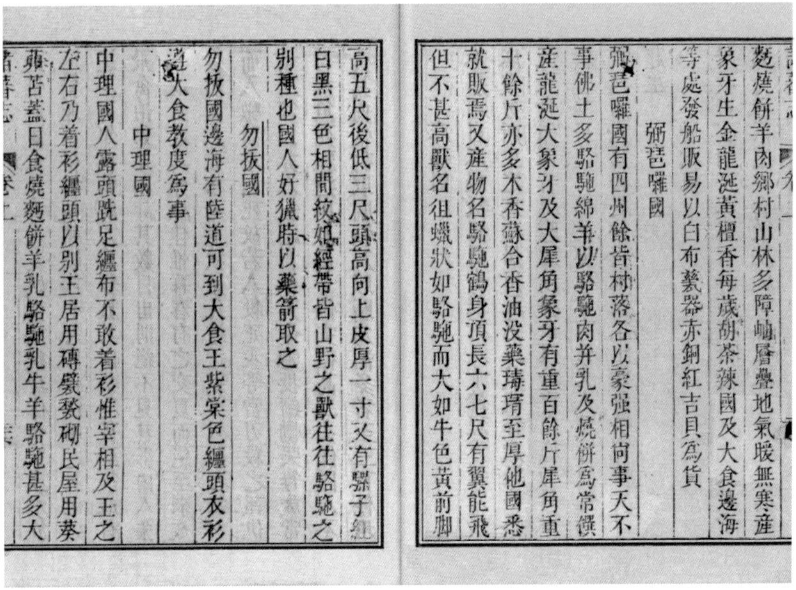

麪燒餅羊肉鄉村山林多障岫層疊地氣暖無寒產
象牙生金龍涎黃檀香每歲胡茶辣國及大食邊海
等處發船販易以白布甆器赤銅紅吉貝爲貨
弼琶囉國
弼琶囉國有四州餘皆村落各以豪強相尚事天不
事佛土多駱駝綿羊以駱駝肉并乳及燒餅爲常饌
產龍涎大象牙及大犀角象牙有重百餘斤犀角重
十餘斤亦多木香蘇合香油沒藥瑇瑁至厚他國悉
就販焉又產物名駱駝鶴身頂長六七尺有翼能飛
但不甚高獸名徂蠟狀如駱駝而大如牛色黃前脚
高五尺後低三尺頭高向上皮厚一寸又有騾子紅
白黑三色相間紋如經帶皆山野之獸往往駱駝之
別種也國人好獵時以藥箭取之
勿拔國
勿拔國邊海有陸道可到大食王紫棠色纏頭衣衫
遵大食教度爲事
中理國
中理國人露頭跣足纏布不敢着衫惟宰相及王之
左右乃着衫纏頭以別王居用磚甓甃砌民屋用葵
茆苫蓋日食燒麪餅羊乳駱駝乳牛羊駱駝甚多大

⦿ Records of Zanzibar in *A Description of Barbarian Nations, Records of Foreign People*

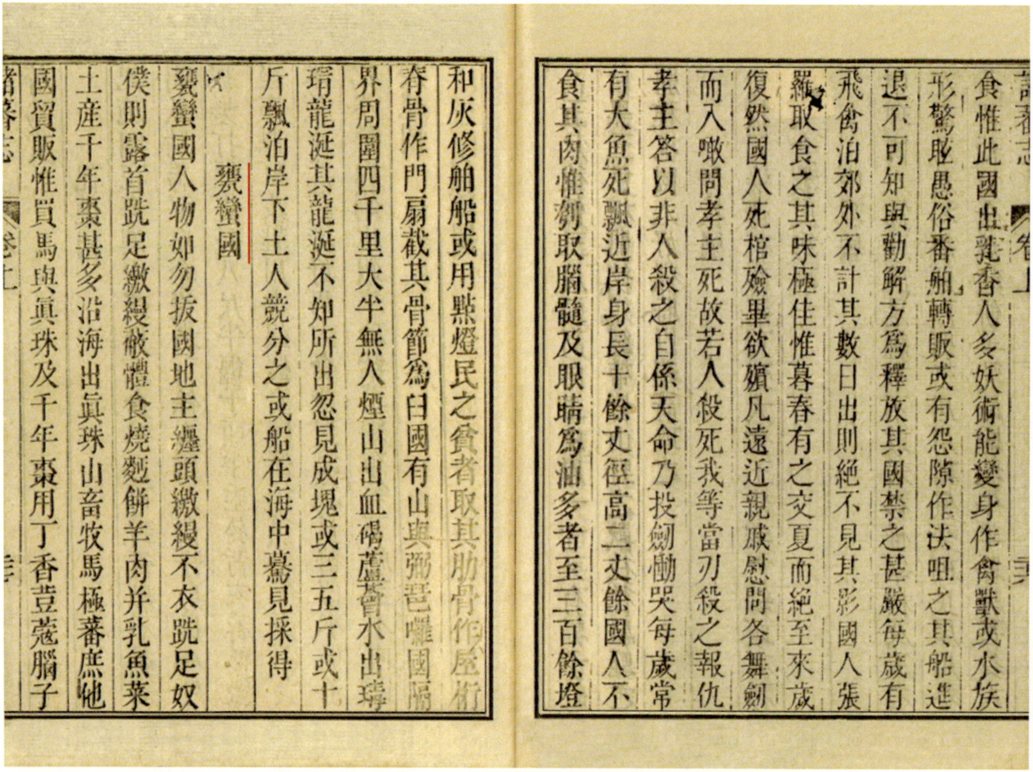

食惟此國出乳香人多妖術能變身作禽獸或水族形驚眩愚俗番舶轉販或有怨隙作法咀之其船進退不可知與勸解方爲釋放其國禁之甚嚴每歲有飛禽泊郊外不計其數日出則絕不見其影國人張羅取食之其味極佳惟暮春有之交夏而絕至來歲復然國人死棺殮畢欲殯凡遠近親戚慰問各舞劍而入嗷問孝主死故若人殺死我等當刃殺之報仇孝主答以非人殺之自係天命乃投劍慟哭每歲常有大魚死飄近岸身長十餘丈徑高二丈餘國人不食其肉惟刳取腦髓及眼睛爲油多者至三百餘墱和灰修舶船或用點燈民之貧者取其肋骨作屋桁脊骨作門扇截其骨節爲臼國有山與弼琶囉國隔界周圍四千里大半無人煙山出血碣蘆薈水出瑇瑁龍涎其龍涎不知所出忽見成塊或三五斤或十斤飄泊岸下土人競分之或船在海中驀見採得

甕蠻國

甕蠻國人物如勿拔國地主纏頭繳縵不衣跣足奴僕則露首跣足繳縵蔽體食燒麪餅羊肉并乳魚菜土產千年棗甚多沿海出眞珠山畜牧馬極蕃庶他國貿販惟買馬與眞珠及千年棗用丁香荳蔻腦子

⦿ Records of Oman in *A Description of Barbarian Nations, Records of Foreign People*

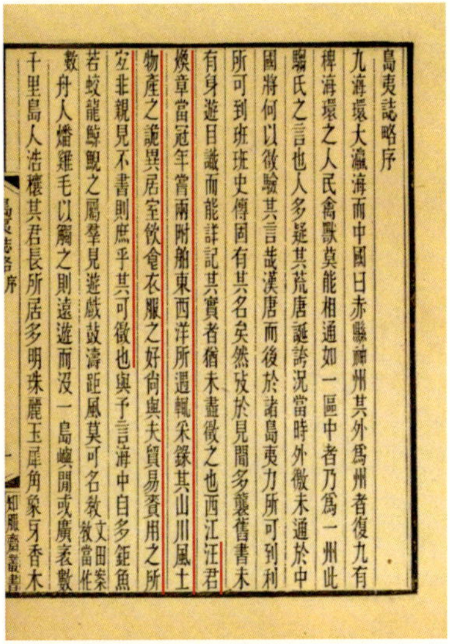
島夷誌略序
九州環大瀛海而中國曰赤縣神州其外為州者復九有
裨海環之人民禽獸莫能相通如一區中者乃為一州此
騶氏之言也人多疑其荒唐誕誇況當時外徼未通於中
國將何以徵驗其言哉漢唐而後於諸島夷力所可到利
所可到班班史傳固有其名矣然考於見聞多襲舊書未
有身遊目識而能詳記其實者猶未盡徵之也西江汪君
煥章當冠年嘗兩附舶東西洋所過輒采錄其山川風土
物產之詭異居室飲食衣服之好尚與夫貿易賚用之所
宜非親見不書則庶乎其可徵也與予言海中自多鉅魚
若蛟龍鯨鯢之屬羣見遊戲鼓濤距風莫可名數文田案數當作
舟人燔雞毛以觸之則遠遊而沒一島嶼間或廣袤數
千里島人浩穰其君長所居多明珠麗玉犀角象牙香木

⦿ Prelude of *A Brief Account of Island Barbarians*, sample page

In the Yuan Dynasty, Wang Dayuan, who was called the "Marco Polo of the East" by Western scholars, set off from Quanzhou twice and sailed east and west. His *A Brief Account of Island Barbarians* records in detail the territory names, customs, and trade of products of over 220 countries and regions. It is an important document for studying the history and geography of China and the West in the Yuan Dynasty

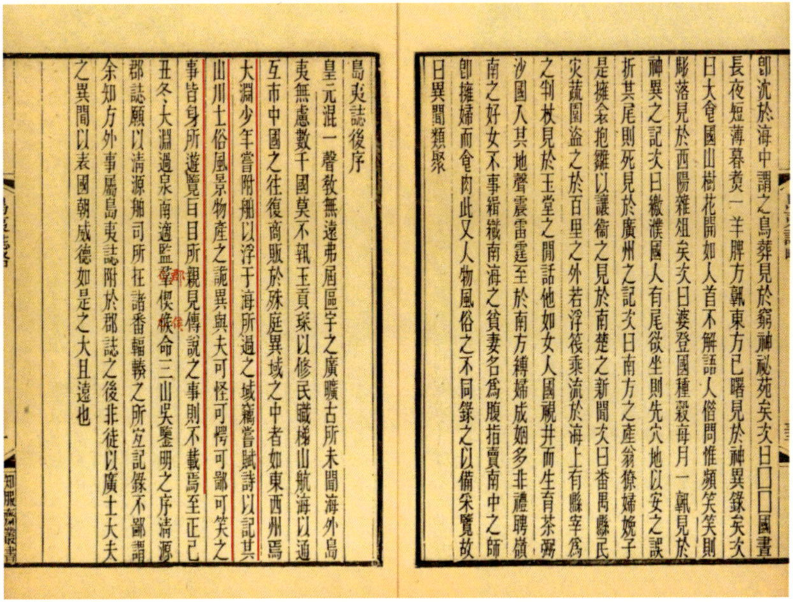
即沉於海中謂之鳥葬見於窮神祕苑矣次曰□□國晝
長夜短薄暮煑一羊胛方熟東方已曙見於神異錄矣次
曰大食國山樹花開如人首不解語人借問惟頻笑笑則
彫落見於酉陽雜俎矣次曰婆登國種穀每月一熟見於
神異之記次曰繳濮國人有尾欲坐則先穴地以安之誤
折其尾則死見於廣州之記次曰南方之產翁獠婦娩子
是擁衾抱雛以讓衛之見於南楚之新聞次曰番禺縣民
灾蔬園盜之於百里之外若浮筏乘流於海上有縣宰為
之判狀見於玉堂之閒話他如女人國覘井而生育茶弼
沙國人其地聲震雷霆至於南方縛婦成姻多非禮聘嶺
南之好女不事紉織南海之貧妻名為腹指賣南中之師
即擁婦而食肉此又人物風俗之不同錄之以備采覽故
曰異聞類聚

島夷誌後序
皇元混一聲教無遠弗屆區宇之廣曠古所未聞海外島
夷無慮數千國莫不執玉貢琛以修民職梯山航海以通
互市中國之往復商販於殊庭異域之中者如東西州焉
大淵少年嘗附舶以浮于海所過之域竊嘗賦詩以記其
山川土俗風景物產之詭異與夫可怪可愕可鄙可笑之
事皆身所遊覽耳目所親見傳說之事則不載焉至正己
丑冬大淵過泉南適監郡偰侯命三山吳鑒明之序清源
郡誌顧以清源舶司所在諸番輻輳之所宜記錄不鄙謂
余知方外事屬島夷誌附於郡誌之後非徒以廣士大夫
之異聞以表國朝威德如是之大且遠也

⦿ Postscript of *A Brief Account of Island Barbarians*, sample page

On October 23, 1990, the UNESCO Maritime Silk Road research ship set sail from Venice, Italy, the hometown of Marco Polo. It arrived in Quanzhou on February 14, 1991, and conducted a five-day comprehensive investigation. It also held the *International Symposium on China and the Maritime Silk Road* at Huaqiao University. Dr. Dean pointed out, "Quanzhou, with a unique position on the Maritime Silk Road, is one of the most important cities in our entire investigation."

⊙ A Maritime Silk Road research ship arrived at Houzhu Port in Quanzhou Bay

CHAPTER 2

The Ancient Rhymes of the Muslims—A Fujian Mosque Tour

The historic buildings allow us to explore distant history. There are mosques in Quanzhou, Shaowu, Fuzhou, and Xiamen. Such mosques not only add cultural landscapes with ethnic characteristics to these cities but also are witnesses of multicultural exchanges.

1 Qingjing Mosque of Quanzhou

During the Song and Yuan dynasties, Quanzhou was world-famous (then called Citong) and was the largest maritime trade port in the East. It had many international nautical and trade connections during this period. Many Arabs came to do business, settled down in Quanzhou along the Maritime Silk Road, and built six or seven mosques. After thousands of years of historic changes, the only remaining mosque in Quanzhou is the Qingjing Mosque, located in the middle of Tumen Street, Licheng District.

Qingjing Mosque, also known as the Shengyou Mosque and the Ashab Mosque, covers an area of 2,184 square meters. Built in 1009, it is one of the oldest remaining mosques in China and the only remaining mosque with a medieval Central Asian architectural style. The main surviving buildings are the gate tower, the worship alter, and the Mingshan Hall. The Qingjing Mosque, Huaihua Mosque of Guangzhou, Phoenix Mosque of Hangzhou, and Xianhe Mosque of Yangzhou are known as the four major mosques in coastal areas of China.

◉ The old image of Qingjing Mosque in Quanzhou of the Republic of China

⦿ Qingjing Mosque in Quanzhou Map in Ming Dynasty (1)

⊙ Qingjing Mosque in Quanzhou Map in Ming Dynasty (2)

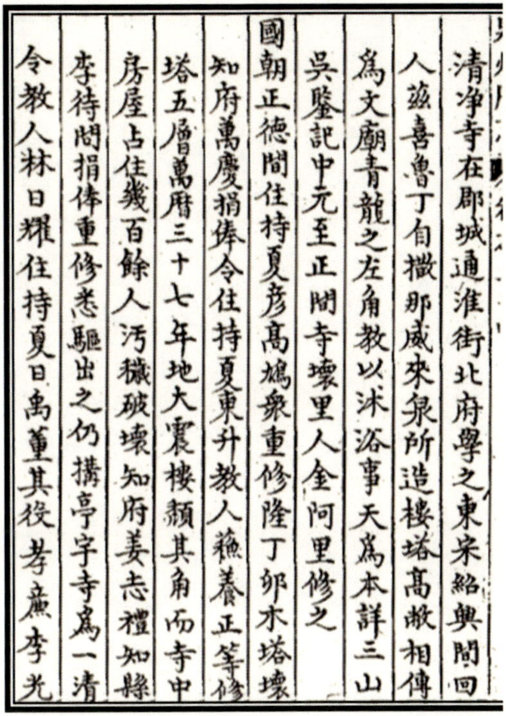

清淨寺在郡城通淮街北府學之東宋紹興間回
人蒳喜魯丁自撒那威來泉所造樓塔高敞相傳
爲文廟青龍之左角教以沭浴事天爲本詳三山
吳鑒記中元至正間寺壞里人金阿里修之
國朝正德間住持夏彦高鳩衆重修隆丁卯木塔壞
知府萬慶捐俸令住持夏東升教人蘓養正等修
塔五層萬曆三十七年地大震樓頽其角而寺中
房屋占住幾百餘人汚穢破壞知府姜志禮知縣
李待問捐俸重修悉驅出之仍搆亭宇寺爲一清
令教人林日耀住持夏日禹董其役孝廉李光

⊙ (LEFT) Records of Qingjing Mosque in *Quanzhou Prefecture Chronicles*, Wanli reign of the Ming Dynasty

⊙ (BELOW) Arabic stone carvings on the back wall of the gate tower of Qingjing Mosque

⦿ Gate of Qingjing

⦿ Gate tower dome of Qingjing Mosque

⦿ (ABOVE) The worship alter in the late Qing Dynasty.

⦿ (RIGHT) The Gate of the worship alter in the Republic of China

⦿ (ABOVE) Aerial view of the worship alter

⦿ (BELOW) Inscriptions on the worship alter

⊙ (LEFT) Mingshan Hall exterior

⊙ (BELOW) Mingshan Hall interior

⊙ One of the four major mosques along the coast, the Qingjing Mosque in Quanzhou

⊙ One of the four major mosques along the coast, the Huaihua Mosque in Guangzhou

◉ One of the four major mosques along the coast, the Phoenix Mosque in Hangzhou

◉ One of the four major mosques along the coast, the Xianhe Mosque in Yangzhou

⊙ Qingjing Mosque Pavilion

⊙ Inscriptions of the imperial edict of the Yongle Emperor

⊙ Arabic stone carvings in the Qingjing Mosque

2 Shaowu Mosque

Shaowu, located in a strategic spot of Fujian, has been a hotly contested spot between military strategists since ancient times. Only Shaowu is home to Hui Muslims in northern Fujian, and Shaowu Mosque is the only mosque in northern Fujian.

The Shaowu Mosque, also known as the Mosque of Worship, resides on Heping Lane, Huaguang Road, Shaowu City. Allegedly, it was built in 1276, and after continuous reconstruction and restoration, it has reached the scale it is today.

Shaowu Mosque is a wooden building. In addition to the hall for chanting, there are affiliated buildings such as the Moon Tower, bungalows, tea rooms, and water rooms. It covers an area of about 3,000 square meters. Its garden layout is Arabic, while its halls have the architectural characteristics of Ming Dynasty China.

⦿ Shaowu Mosque

⊙ (ABOVE) The entrance hall couplet

⊙ (LEFT) The Moon Tower

⊙ (BELOW) Tian Fang Gu Jiao Plaque

⦿ Arabic gate top

⦿ Carved stone pillar

⦿ Zhen You Wu Xiang Plaque

3 Fuzhou Mosque

Historically, as the long-time political center of Fujian, Fuzhou has been highly valued by the rulers of the past dynasties. Thus, it gained a unique advantage in conducting overseas exchanges. During the Yuan and Ming Dynasties, it also became one of the places where Arabs and Persians engaged in business and mission activities.

Fuzhou Mosque, located on Bayiqi North Road, Fuzhou City, covers an area of about 2,300 square meters. According to the inscription Reconstruction of the Mosque, made in the mosque in 1549, it was built in 628, rebuilt in 1541, and completed eight years later. The reconstructed mosque has the traditional style of quadrangle dwellings, with the mosque in the center, tea room on the left, corridor and kitchen on the right, and ornamental columns opposite the mosque.

Fuzhou Mosque was the only place for Muslims to worship Allah in Fuzhou. In 2009, the Fuzhou Municipal Government decided to rebuild it comprehensively. The reconstruction officially started in 2013 and was completed in 2015.

⊙ Fuzhou Mosque

⊙ The old gate of Fuzhou Mosque

⊙ Arabic on the gate top

⦿ Exterior

⦿ Interior

⊙ Copper incense burner

⊙ Xian Yang Sheng Jiao Plaque

⊙ Stone balustrade in front of the mosque

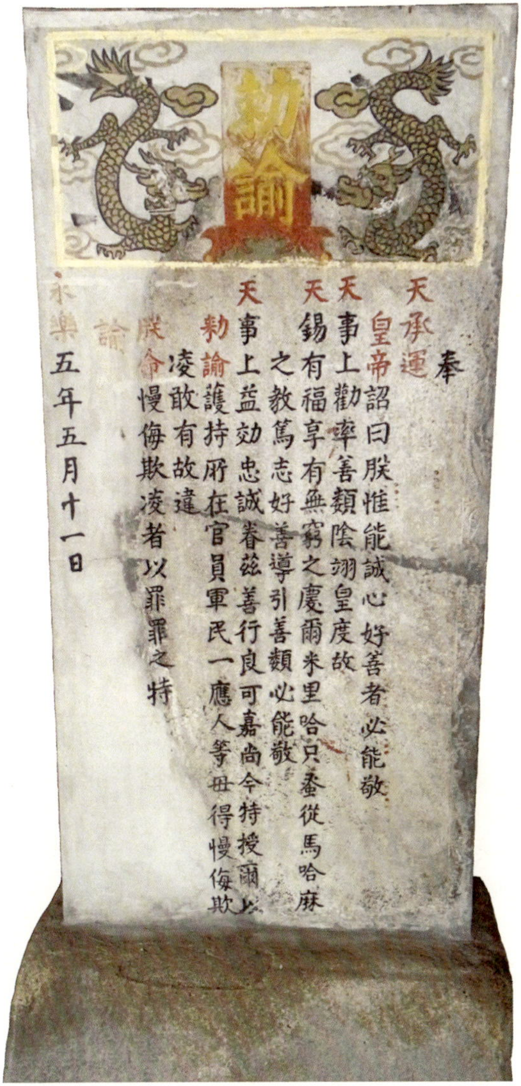

⊙ Inscriptions of the Imperial Edict of Yongle

⊙ The Reconstruction of the Mosque inscription

4 Xiamen Mosque

Initially located on Yuping Lane, Park South Road, the Xiamen Mosque was built in 1823. It was the first mosque in Xiamen.

The Xiamen Mosque at first had only one hall and one courtyard. During the Emperor Tongzhi's reign (1862–1875). The Commander of Xiamen's Defense advocated the expansion of the front building and the addition of walls, forming the traditional Chinese architectural pattern of a front hall, a central hall, and a main hall. The mosque sits west to east, with a total construction area of 2,365 square meters. In 1896, Yang Qizhen, the Admiral of the Fujian Navy, donated four shops to the mosque, which was recorded in the Xiamen Mosque Inscription that has survived to this day.

An old image of the Xiamen Mosque

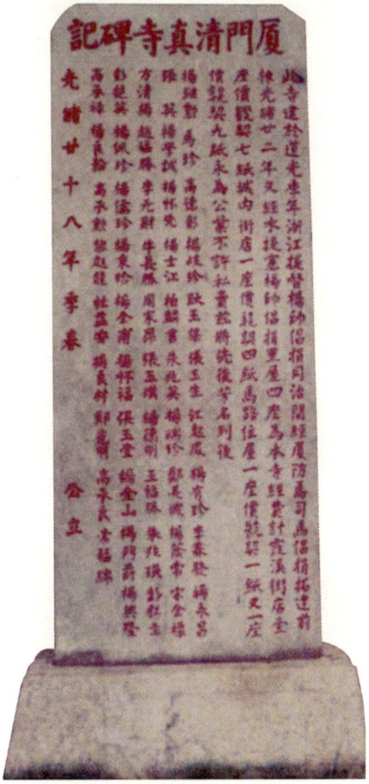

◉ 1902 Xiamen Mosque inscription

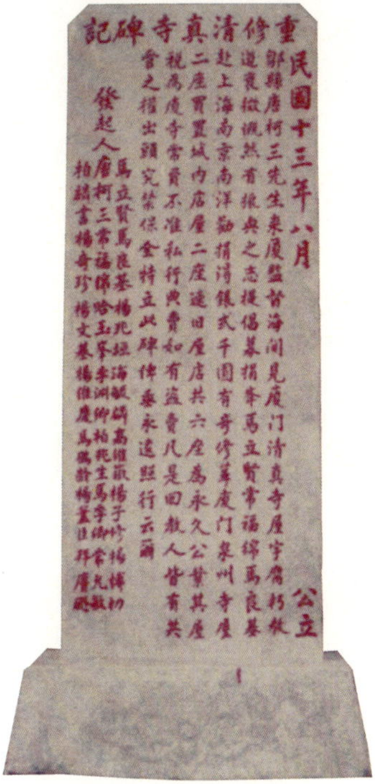

◉ 1924 Reconstruction of the Xiamen Mosque inscription

The Xiamen People's Government granted funds in 1955 to repair the Xiamen Mosque, and from 1982 to 1987, it was fully renovated in two phases. In June 1988, the entire renovation project was complete. In July 1993, it was completely demolished for reconstruction and relocated to 27-29 Park South Road (about 50 meters away from the old site), and it was completed and reopened in October 2003. The new mosque is a six-story building imitating the Arabian style, with a total construction area of 2,400 square meters. It is now the center of religious activities for Chinese and foreign Muslims in the Xiamen Special Economic Zone.

⦿ The front door of Xiamen Mosque after repairs in the early 1980s

⦿ A birds-eye view of the fully renovated Xiamen Mosque in 1988

CHAPTER 3

Eternal Memory—Stories of the Islamic Tombstones

The Chinese have a tradition of carving stones to record history. Many Arabs and Persians who sailed across the sea to Fujian in the past settled there and even died there, leaving behind many sarcophagi (coffins) and tombstones. By interpreting these tombstone inscriptions, we can confirm the past's facts and correct the errors in historical documents. Every tombstone inscription of Arabs, Persians, and their descendants that remain in Fujian records the story of a person or a family, allowing us to explore the stories of Arabs and Persians who traveled across the ocean to Fujian.

1 Arabian Carved Stones in Quanzhou

Although most of the Muslim graveyards in Quanzhou during the Song and Yuan Dynasties have been destroyed, some tomb covers and tombstones with beautifully carved Islamic patterns and inscriptions that record the names of the deceased, date of birth and death, place of origin, and verses from the Koran and Hadith (the collected traditions of the Prophet Muhammad, based on his sayings and actions) in Arabic, Persian and Chinese have survived. They are essential materials for exploring the historic exchanges between Quanzhou and the Arab world. They witnessed Quanzhou's prosperity in maritime transportation and multicultural harmony from the 10th to the 14th century.

The Islamic exhibition hall of the Quanzhou Maritime Museum displays many Arabic-style tombstones, which were widely distributed in Jintoupu, Puxi, Yuanqian, and Houban in Quanzhou. In 1998, over 60 Islamic tomb covers and components of mosques built by Yemenis were excavated in Jintoupu area, which suggests that it was once an important settlement and burial area for Arabs.

⦿ A special exhibition, Arab-Persians in Quanzhou, in the Quanzhou Maritime Museum

⊙ The stele in the "Arab-Persian in Quanzhou" exhibition hall of the Quanzhou Maritime Museum

⊙ The excavation site of the components of the Jintoupu Mosque and tomb covers in Quanzhou in 1998

The earliest known Arabic tombs in Quanzhou are the Holy Islamic Tombs on the southern side of Lingshan Mountain in Quanzhou. In this burial area, which covers an area of about 300 square meters, rests two disciples of the Islamic prophet Muhammad who came to Quanzhou to preach during the Wude period of the Tang Dynasty (618–626). These tombs are Islamic Sumeru-style tombs carved from two granite blocks juxtaposed in the east and west. They are rectangular and face the south. Inside and outside the tomb corridor are seven inscriptions of past dynasties. There are five steles in the corridor. On the center stele is written "Holy Tombs Rebuilt," and it was made in 1322. It briefly describes the stories of two disciples of the Islamic prophet Muhammad in Arabic; on the right is a stele with Chinese inscriptions erected by Zheng He when he passed Quanzhou on his way to the West in 1417 and paid tribute to his ancestors. These inscriptions are important cultural relics for studying Chinese Islam and the history of these tombs.

⦿ Holy Islamic Tombs of Lingshan

⦿ The stele in Arabic, "Holy Tombs Rebuilt," in 1322

⦿ The prayer Stele of Zheng He in 1417

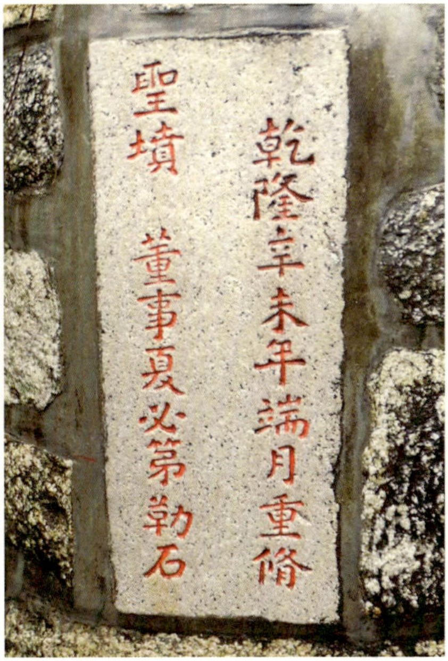

⦿ The stele of Xia Bidi rebuilding the holy tombs in 1751

⦿ The stele of Guo Bacui rebuilding the holy tombs in 1783

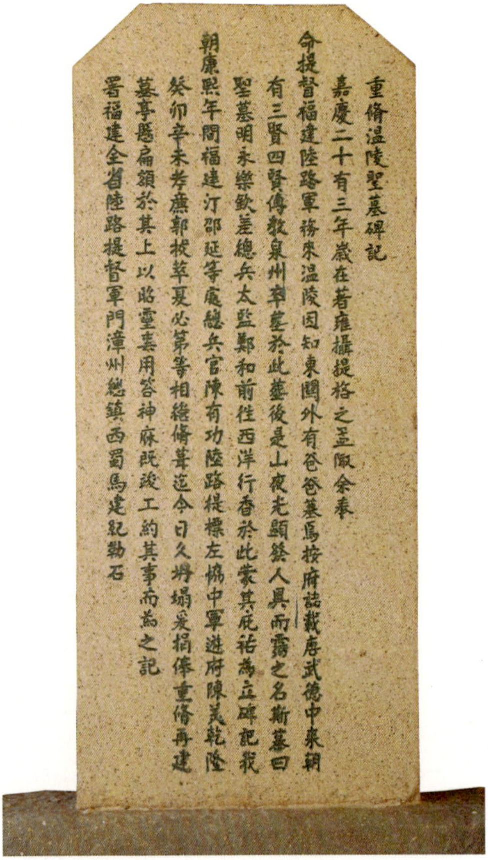

⊙ The stele of Ma Jianji rebuilding the holy tombs of Wenling in 1818

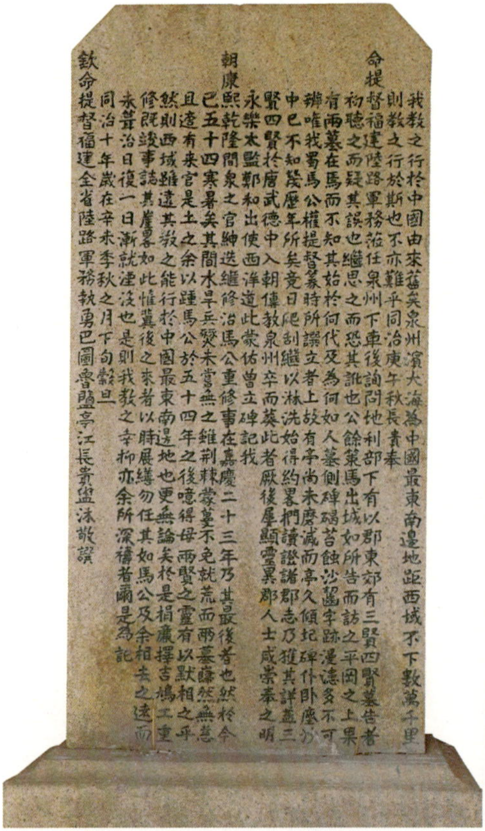

⊙ The stele of Jiang Changgui rebuilding the holy tombs in 1871

Iranian experts Ali Sakhawat and Natali believe that in the Islamic world, in addition to the Holy Tomb of Muhammad and the Holy Tomb of Ali, the tombs of the two disciples of the Islamic prophet Muhammad in Quanzhou are the oldest and most valuable. As one of the earliest areas where Islam was introduced into China, Quanzhou remains home to tens of thousands of Arab descendants and retains strong Islamic cultural traditions and numerous historical sites.

⊙ In 1991, UNESCO experts inspected the Holy Islamic Tombs in Quanzhou

On November 20, 1926, Chen Wanli, a famous Chinese ceramics expert and archaeology instructor at the School of Chinese Studies at Xiamen University, and his entourage came to the Dongchan Temple by the East Lake outside Renfeng Gate, Quanzhou. They discovered many Arabic sarcophagi near the temple. His notes of that day in his book *Journey to Southern Fujian* record the sarcophagus patterns and the location of these tombstones in detail. And the photos were taken at that time clearly show the original style of the tombs.

⊙ Arabic sarcophagi near Dongcan Temple

Quanzhou Maritime Museum displays tomb covers collected from all over Quanzhou.

The tower-type stone tomb cover of the Yuan Dynasty displayed in the Islamic Exhibition Hall belongs to Mahmoud bin Mohammed bin Abu Bashri Gilani, who was from Jilan in northern Iran. The tombstone, made of an

⊙ A set of tower-type stone tomb covers

⊙ The stone tomb covers in the Quanzhou Maritime Museum

entire solid diabase monolith, is divided into four layers. Ruyi cloud patterns are engraved between the six feet on the bottom layer, a lotus petal pattern is engraved on the second, and a circle of Arabic script is embossed on the third. The top stone's cross-section is shaped like a pointed arch. On one end, there is a pattern of clouds embracing the full moon; on the other, it is a pattern of a blooming lotus.

⊙ Yuan Dynasty Muhammad tower-type stone tomb cover

⊙ Part of the Yuan Dynasty Muhammad tower-type stone tomb cover

⦿ The capstone of the Yuan Dynasty Islamic tower-type stone tomb cover with a new crescent pattern

⦿ Part of the capstone of the Yuan Dynasty Islamic tower-type stone tomb cover with a new crescent pattern

The exhibition hall has one exceptional capstone, a tower-type stone tomb cover with cloud and moon patterns. Different from the full moon pattern on the other stone tomb covers, the pattern at one end of this tombstone is a crescent moon embraced by cirrus clouds. This is the only one with such a pattern in Quanzhou. The crescent moon, a commonly used decorative pattern in the buildings and flags of Islamic countries, symbolizes rising and prosperity.

In 1972, a Yuan Dynasty Islamic Sumeru-style shawl stone tomb cover was discovered in the west graveyard of Fashimei Mountain, Quanzhou. There was no Arabic text or tombstone when the tomb cover was discovered, so we cannot tell who the tomb's owner was. However, based on such exquisite decoration and carving, the owner must have been a noble, perhaps an Arab lady.

⊙ Yuan Dynasty Islamic Sumeru-style shawl stone tomb cover

⊙ Part of the Yuan Dynasty Islamic Sumeru-style shawl stone tomb cover

In addition to the tower-type stone tombs mentioned above, there is also an altar-type stone tomb in Quanzhou, which can be confirmed by the many retaining stones that have survived. Wu Wenliang once restored the line drawing of the corset-style altar-type stone tomb. The entire stone tomb is often carved from dozens of diabase (a dark gray to black, fine-grained, igneous rock) or granite. In the center of the tomb, on top stands a pointed, arched tombstone, mainly with pattern clouds supporting the moon. And the middle of the moon is engraved in Arabic, and the content is mostly the name and date of the birth and death of the tomb owner or verses from the Koran. The tomb is shaped like a rectangular altar, whose upper and lower stone slabs protrude, and the transition is lotus petals or lotus petal patterns. The middle waist is composed of three-to-five square retaining stones, inscribed with Arabic or carved with cloud-moon patterns. The connection between the retaining stones is decorated with column partitions, with cloud patterns or intertwined flower patterns at the bottom. And the bottom layer is supported by six ruyi-patterned feet.

⦿ Restored line drawing of a corset-style altar-type stone tomb

⊙ Yuan Dynasty Islamic Du'ansha retaining stone

⊙ Yuan Dynasty Islamic Bukharian retaining stone

Based on tombstone components and fieldwork, Chen Dasheng restored another style of Chinese altar tombs, a new form combining Islamic style with traditional Chinese tombs. This kind of tomb comprises a tomb ring, tomb hands, pillars, mounds, altar, isosceles trapezoid tombstones, and retaining stone carvings. Similar to the corset-style altar-type stone tomb, the retaining stone is also placed in the corset, and the isosceles trapezoid tombstone is put in front of the mound.

In the preserved tombs of the Ding family in Chendai, who were Arab descendants, the combination of Arab tombs and Chinese tombs can be seen. And the tower-type stone tomb cover of Ding Fubao, the fifth-generation ancestor of the Ding family in Chendai, adopts the Arabic style, which is proof that it was integrated with Chinese tomb styles. This is a kind of typical presentation of the cultural exchange between China and the Arab world.

⊙ The tower-type stone tomb cover of Ding Fubao, the fifth-generation ancestor of the Ding family in Chendai

In addition to these exquisite stone tomb covers, there are several rough stone tomb covers on the grass outside the exhibition hall. These were excavated at the end of Tumen Street. There was a workshop specializing in making and processing stone tomb covers. However, judging from the number of existing stone tomb covers, there must have been more than one such stone workshop during the hundreds of years of the Song and Yuan Dynasties, and artisans may have abandoned these unfinished stone tomb covers during the change of dynasties.

⦿ The rough stone material of a stone tomb cover on the grass of the Quanzhou Maritime Museum

In the Islam Exhibition Hall, several tombstones engraved with both Arabic and Chinese texts are the most eye-catching. On one of them, three Chinese characters, *Fan Ke Mu* (*Tomb of Foreigners*) were written. It was unearthed in 1965 in the southeast corner of Jincuowei on the west slope of Dongyue Mountain in Quanzhou. However, two of the three Chinese characters are incorrectly written, but the Arabic is written correctly. Perhaps the person inscribed on the tombstone was an expatriate who had just started living in Quanzhou. Having learned some basic Chinese characters, he imitated the tombstone of the Han Chinese and added these three characters to Arabic texts. From another perspective, the simple and innocent brushwork confirms the cultural exchanges in those years.

⊙ The tombstone where *Tomb of Foreigners* was written

Among the tombstones engraved with Chinese characters, we also notice that the owners of two tombstones used to be officials, namely the tombstone of commander Pan and the tombstone of Lu Huachi, head of Yongchun County. And the tombstone engraved with commander Pan has Chinese inscriptions on both sides in the Arabic texts. The Chinese texts are "Commander Pan died on April 1" while the Arabic is "Except him, everything is doomed. He judges while you are only called to him." We can't tell what specific official position the commander was, but it should be within the jurisdiction of Quanzhou at the time.

⦿ The tombstone of commander Pan

⦿ The double-sided tombstone of Lu Huachi, scholar-official and head of Yongchun County

In addition to the tombstones with Chinese and Arabic inscriptions, most of the surviving monuments have only Arabic inscriptions. After scholars translated them, it was discovered that the owners of these tombstones came from Isfahan, Bukhara, Armenia, Sīrāf, Yemen, and other places.

In 1965, a tombstone with six lines of Arabic texts inscribed on one side was discovered at the infrastructure construction site in Quanzhou City. And it was identified as the tombstone of Hussein bin Mohammad Khalat in 1171. Khalat was the capital of Armenia, an ancient country in Central Asia.

⊙ Tombstone of Hussein bin Muhammad Khalat

Many of the surviving Arabic tombstones in Quanzhou belong to female owners. The tombstone of Amir Tughesun Amir Ali bin Hassan bin Ali Gurusi is unique because it is the only tombstone with Arabic inscriptions on its front, back, and both sides.

Tombstone of Fatimah, daughter of Moses

Component of the tombstone of Fatimah, daughter of Hamid ed-Din

Tombstone of the daughter of Said Bourtoma

Remaining inscriptions of the Song Dynasty are rare, and most tombstones came from the Yuan Dynasty. From this, we can speculate that most of the Muslims who came to Quanzhou in the Song Dynasty were transient, while in the Yuan Dynasty, many Muslims settled down. Although we do not know how many Arabs and Persians traveled to Quanzhou during the Song and Yuan Dynasties and how many of them were buried there, the surviving hundreds of stone inscriptions prove the close interaction between China and Persia and the Arab world.

⦿ Double-sided tombstone of Amir Tughesun

2 Islamic Tombs in Shaowu and Fuzhou

Compared with the more prosperous historical sites and tombstone cultural relics in Quanzhou, there are far fewer Islamic tombs in Shaowu and Fuzhou. However, scholars have found some historic relics in the mountains.

In Shaowu, a city in the north of Fujian, there was once a famous saying that half the citizens are Hui people. Now, in addition to the remaining mosques, there are still hundreds of Muslim tombs on Huilong Mountain.

For historic reasons, we now can see tombs since the Qing Dynasty, many of which were built after the founding of the People's Republic of China. Allegedly, it is challenging to find tombs of the Yuan and Ming dynasties on this mountain because there have been multiple relocations of the burial areas. Perhaps because of the times, or the difference in the birthplaces of the tomb owners, the Muslim tombs in Shaowu clearly differ from those in Quanzhou.

⦿ A Hui tomb in Shaowu

Judging from the surviving tombs, Muslim tombs in Shaowu have relatively simple shapes. Some are just a mound, and some use stone bars, but even so, they are not like the stone tomb covers in Quanzhou, which have intricate patterns and Arabic inscriptions.

⦿ A Hui tombstone in Shaowu

Near the West Lake in Fuzhou, next to Jingbianting Village at the northern foot of Xiangshan Mountain, there is a hill called the General Tomb of Muslims, which is the cemetery area of Fuzhou Muslims. The tomb shapes and tombstones preserved suggest most of the tombstones were made in the Qing Dynasty, except for a few in the Ming Dynasty.

The most eye-catching is a Yuan Dynasty tomb called the Saint's Tomb. And the Arabic texts of the stone door frame and the lintel confirm that the tomb owner was the famous Islamic missionary Ibn Marjad Amir Al-Din, who died in 1306. And the shape of the stone tomb cover suggests it was made in the Yuan Dynasty, and the inscriptions state that it was repaired in the Ming and Qing dynasties. In 1983, the Fuzhou Municipal People's Government designated this tomb in the second batch of municipal-level cultural relics protection units and renovated it.

⦿ The gate of the Xiangshan Muslim Cemetery in Fuzhou

⦿ The shape of a Muslim tomb in Fuzhou

⦿ Modern Muslim tombs in Fuzhou

CHAPTER 4

Ancestral Memory—Muslim Descendants in Quanzhou

With the prosperity of overseas trade and the opening of sea routes, many Arabs and Persians came to the coastal city of Fujian via the Maritime Silk Road, and some settled there. As time goes by, finding Arab descendants in Fuzhou has become challenging, while there are still some families of Arab and Persian Muslim descendants in Quanzhou.

Among the Muslim families in Quanzhou, the Pu family, the Ding family, and the Guo family are the biggest, and they have gradually formed distinctive settlements as time went by. Although these Muslim descendants have continued to integrate into the local culture of Quanzhou for hundreds of years, they have also tried to maintain their foreign cultural traditions.

1 The Pu family of Quanzhou

The family of Pu Shougeng was the most influential Muslim family in Quanzhou during the Song and Yuan dynasties. His Arab ancestors first settled in Guangzhou. When Quanzhou Port gradually prospered, the Pu family moved from Guangzhou to Quanzhou. There are records of Pu Shougeng in the *Book of Fujian* and *Dong Wenbing Shen Dao Bei*.

The Pu family owned many sea ships and had close business contacts with foreign countries, which has accumulated great wealth for the Pu descendants. The family's strong maritime performance and prominent power made it a giant in the wealthy Quanzhou city at that time. They enabled it to have a political right of speech locally. Throughout the Yuan Dynasty, the Pu family was always distinguished in Quanzhou, which engaged in overseas trade.

Quanzhou still retains place names related to Pu Shougeng, such as Chessboard Garden, Banpu Street, Daaimen, and more. Allegedly, these places used to be part of his mansion. There are also relics of the footprints of the Pu family in Qingyuan Mountain and Fashi. The inscription titled *Reconstruction of Chunyang Cave of Qingyuan* on the cliff in Chunyang Cave of Qingyuan Mountain records that Pu Shougeng once served as a manager of government affairs in Fujian Province. Historically, the Wanghai Tower of Haiyin Temple was built for Pu to watch the ships entering and leaving the port.

⊙ *Stories of Pu Shougeng*, by Jitsuzō Kuwabara, Chinese translation, sample page

⊙ An inscription, Reconstruction of Chunyang Cave of Qingyuan

⊙ Haiyin Temple

At the end of the Yuan Dynasty, the ten-year-long Yisibaxi War broke out, completely changing Quanzhou's original local political situation. The Arabs living in Quanzhou left one after another or stayed away from the city and hid in the countryside. In the early years of the Ming Dynasty, the government even formulated a policy to prevent Pu's descendants from studying and becoming officials. The Pu family, which was thriving, faded away.

According to the survey, the descendants of the Pu family were distributed in the urban area of Quanzhou, Jinjiang, Yongchun, Anxi, Dehua, Fuzhou, Zhangpu, Zhao'an, and many other places outside Fujian Province during the Ming and Qing Dynasties. And they recorded the family changes through their family pedigree, which they learned from the Chinese.

⦿ The ancestral hall of the Pu family

⦿ The memorial tablets of the Pu ancestors

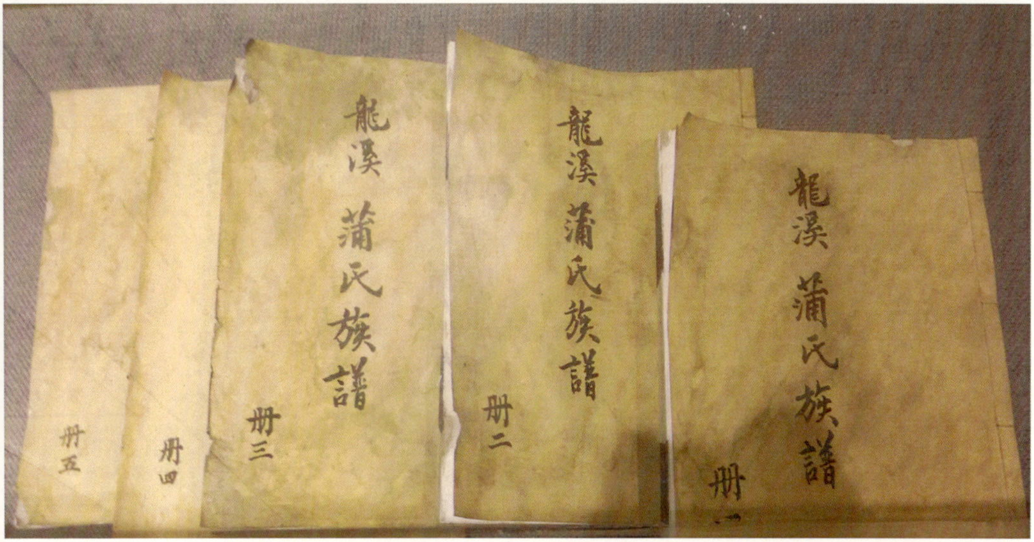

⊙ The Pu family tree

⊙ Hedong Yanpai, a brand of the Pu family

Since the production and trade of perfume was the Pu family's principal business, the descendants of the Pu family who moved out of the city center inherited the tradition of their ancestors, planting flowers and making perfume. The Pu descendants in Hankou Village, Dapu Town, Yongchun County, produced perfume to be exported overseas. They even opened the Perfume Shop of Pu Qinglan, which specialized in making *mie* perfume. And Dapu Town has also won the reputation of the "Capital of Fragrance," due to its long history of perfume making and the economic prosperity of its perfume industry.

⊙ The golden signboard of the Perfume Shop of Pu Qinglan

⊙ Seal of Qinglan Perfume

⊙ The old scale of the Perfume Shop of Pu Qinglan

2 The Ding Family of Chendai

More than 700 years ago, the ancestors of the Ding family came from West Asia via the Maritime Silk Road to Fujian. Excellent at business operations, they combined Islamic and Chinese cultures, forming a unique clan that integrated Chinese and Islamic culture—the Hui people surnamed Ding.

The main settlement of the Ding family is Chendai Town, Jinjiang City, Fujian Province. More than 20,000 Ding family members are distributed in the seven administrative villages of Jiangtou, Andou, Xibian, Sijing, Huatingkou, Pengtou, and Xiban. They are called "the thousands of Dings." According to the genealogy of the Ding family, the Ding ancestors came to Quanzhou from Suzhou for business at the end of the Song Dynasty. Since the Yuan Dynasty, they moved to Chendai and settled there.

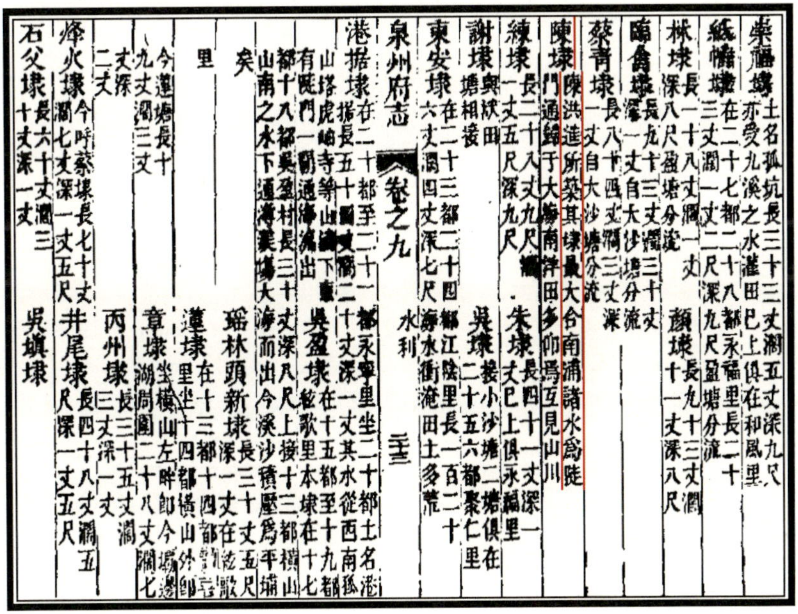

⦿ Records of Chendai in *Quanzhou Prefecture Chronicles*

Thousands of Dings in Chendai plaque

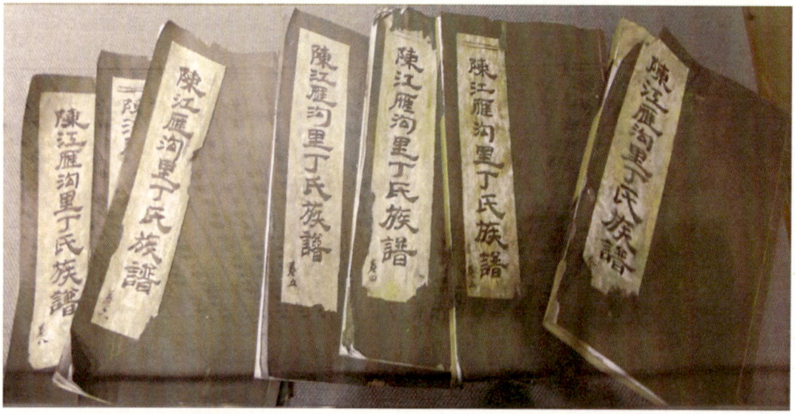

Genealogy of the Ding family in Yangou, Chenjiang

(FAR LEFT) Statue of the first-generation ancestor of the Ding family, Ding Jiezhai

(LEFT) Statue of the fourth-generation ancestor of the Ding family, Ding Ren'an

The identification of the Dings in Chendai as Muslim can be confirmed from the *Ancestral History* in their genealogy and the records of the ancestral rituals. The *Ancestral History of the Ding Family* records that the family follows Islam and Islamic customs. In 1699, Ding Qing wrote *Records of Rituals*, which details the Ding family's ancestral rituals and mentions the identification of their Hui ethnicity multiple times.

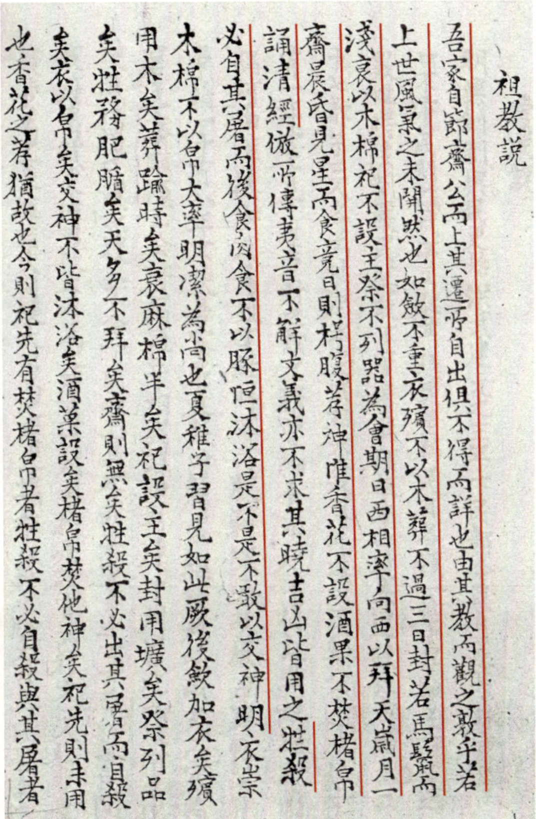

⊙ *Ancestral History*, sample page

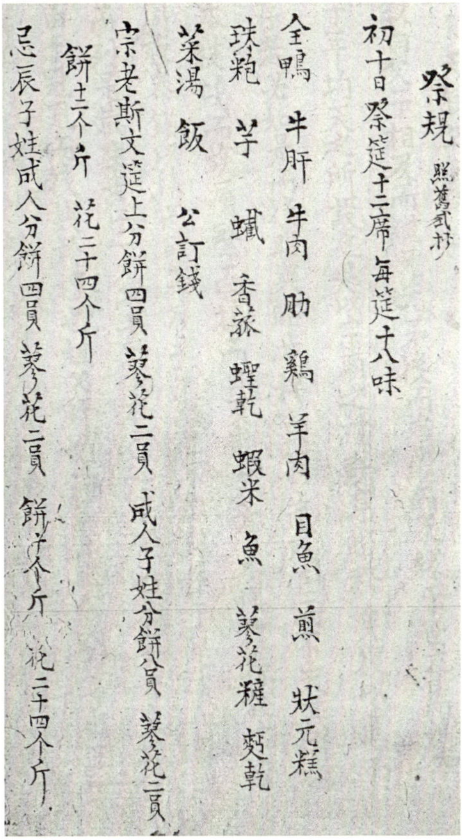

⊙ *Rules of Rituals*, sample page

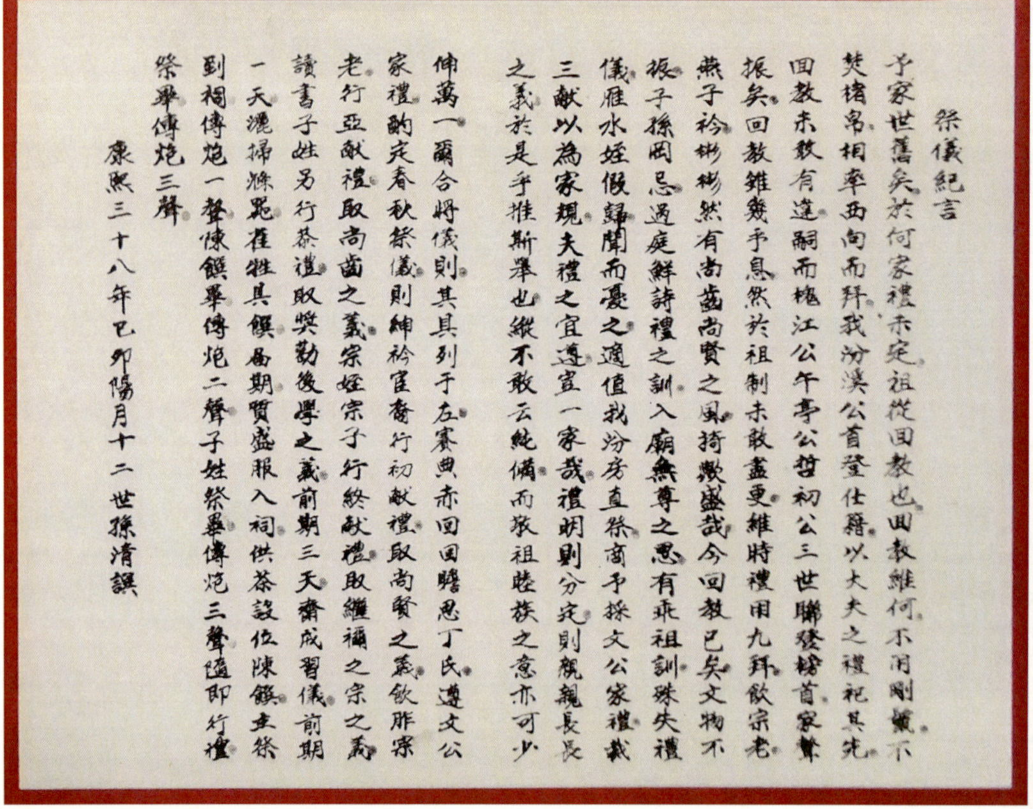

祭儀紀言

予家世舊矣於何家禮未定祖從回教也回教維何不用刪黨不焚楮帛相率西向而拜我汾溪公首登仕籍以大夫之禮祀其先回教未戢有蓮嗣而梅江公午亭公哲初公三世聯登榜首家聲振矣回教雖幾乎息然於祖制未敢盡更維時禮用九拜飲宗老燕子衿彬彬然有尚齒尚賢之風猗歟盛哉今回教已矣文物不振子孫罔忌過庭鮮詩禮之訓入廟無尊之思有乖祖訓殊失禮儀雁水姪假歸聞而憂之適值我汾房直祭商予採文公家禮載三獻以為家規夫禮之宜適宜一家哉禮明則分定則親親長長之義於是乎推斯舉也縱不敢云純備而報祖睦族之意亦可少伸萬一爾合將儀則其具列于左賽典亦回回瞻思丁氏遵文公家禮酌定春秋祭儀則紳衿宜奮行初獻禮取尚賢之義飲胙宗老行亞獻禮取尚齒之義宗姪宗子行終獻禮取繼禰之宗之義讀書子姓另行恭讀取獎勸後學之義前期三天齋戒習儀前期一天灑掃滌器省牲具饌届期質盛服入祠供茶設位陳饌主祭到祠傳炮一聲陳饌畢傳炮二聲子姓祭畢傳炮三聲隨即行禮祭畢傳炮三聲

康熙三十八年己卯陽月十二世孫清譔

⦿ *Records of Rituals*, sample page

Since the Ming Dynasty, the Ding descendants studied hard for the imperial examinations, and many became court officials, generals, poets, scientists, and local gentry. Among them, Ding Gongchen, a military firearms scientist in the late Qing Dynasty, was the most well-known.

Ding Gongchen (1800–1875), who was accomplished in the study of military firearms, is known as a famous patriotic military scientist in modern times. During his lifetime, he authored *Illustrated Artillery*, *Illustrated Artillery II*, *Zeng Bu Ze Ke Lu*, *Illustrations of Western Arms*, *Illustrations of Western Steamers and Steamships*, and other works. Among them, *Illustrated Artillery* was highly recommended by Wei Yuan and Lin Zexu.

⊙ Portrait of Ding Gongchen

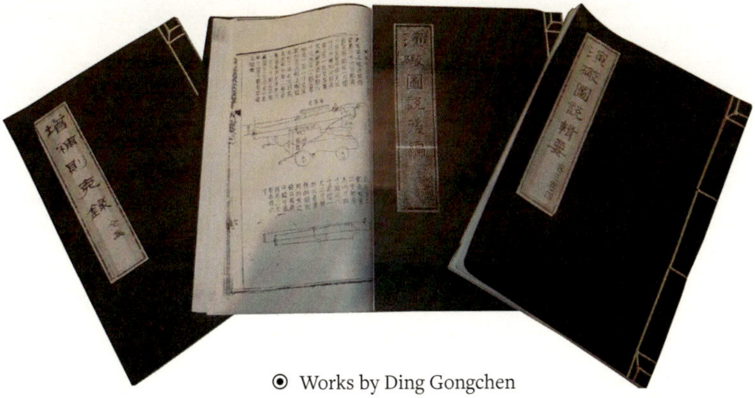

⊙ Works by Ding Gongchen

⦿ World-Famous plaque

⦿ Cannons collected in Ding's ancestral hall

Influenced by Confucian culture, the Ding family formed a Hui literati association called *Peng Xiao Xie*. They also accepted Han culture, built ancestral halls like the Han Chinese, and compiled genealogies. The pictures depicting their ancestors' lives show that they fully blended into the Han Chinese.

⦿ *Peng Xiao Xie*, sample page

⊙ The Ding family's ancestral hall in Andou Village, Chendai Town (old photo)

⊙ The Ding family's ancestral hall in Andou Village, Chendai Town (new photo)

⦿ (RIGHT) A painting of the Ding ancestors' life

⦿ (BELOW) The Ding residence with a lintel upon which is written *Ju Shu Yan Pai (Be Educated and Raise a Family)*

⦿ (ABOVE) The Ding family's ancestral hall

⦿ (LEFT) The stone pillar couplet at the Ding family's ancestral hall

⦿ The memorial tablets at the Ding family's ancestral hall

According to statistics, in the Ming and Qing dynasties, 12 descendants from the Ding family in Chendai became *jinshi* (*"advanced scholar"*), 21 became *juren* (*"recommended man"*), 26 became *gongsheng* (*"tribute student"*), and 105 became *xiucai* (*"distinguished scholar"*), repeatedly honoring the family. The Ding family had a strong sense of patriotism and loved their hometown. During the War of Resistance Against Japanese Aggression in 1941, the Ding people traveling in the Philippines raised funds and donated planes to support the motherland. Therefore, the National Government rewarded them with a plaque that stated: "Loyal Defenders of the Country."

⦿ Father and Son, both *jinshi* plaque

⦿ Loyal defender of the country Plaque

On the east side of the Holy Islamic Tomb of Lingshan resides the tomb group of the Ding of Chendai. Judging from the shape of the tombs, the surrounding horse-hoof-shaped tomb circle is a typical feature of Han tombs in Fujian, and a stone tomb cover is placed in front of the tomb circle, which maintains the Arabic tradition.

⦿ Tombs of the Ding family of Chendai, Jinjiang

⦿ The joint tomb of the first, second, and third generations of Ding ancestors of Chenjiang

⦿ Memorial gate of the joint tomb of the Ding ancestors of Chendai (front)

⦿ Memorial gate of the joint tomb of the Ding ancestors of Chendai (back)

⦿ Memorial Pavilion

⊙ Fourth-generation ancestor of the Ding Family of Chendai, Ding Shan (Ren'an) and his wife Zhuang's Tombs

◉ Tower-type stone tomb covers of Ding Guanbao, Ding Kuan, Ding Min, the fifth-generation and sixth-generation ancestors of the Ding Family of Chendai

◉ The tombs of Ding Yi'an, the fifth-generation ancestor of the Ding family of Chenjiang, his first wife Pu, and second wife Wang

Behind Ding's ancestral hall is a two-story mosque, which is the Islamic center of Jinjiang and Shishi. And the current Jinjiang Islamic Association is located in this mosque.

The genealogy, the tomb shape, the mosque, and the historical materials of the Ding family prove that this family had a deep relationship with Arab Muslims.

◉ Mosque gate of Chendai, Jinjiang

◉ (LEFT) Mosque of Chendai, Jinjiang

◉ (ABOVE) Jinjiang Islamic Association

3 The Guo Family of Baiqi

Baiqi, known as Baiqipu in ancient times, is the only Hui township among the 19 ethnic minority townships in Fujian Province and the only ethnic minority township in Quanzhou City. There are still a large number of Islamic cultural relics and historical sites in Baiqi Township, telling the history of the integration of Arabs and Chinese.

There are over 15,000 Guo family members living in Baiqi Hui Township. According to their genealogy, the ancestors of the Guo family were Arab Muslims who came to China for business along the Maritime Silk Road. They came to Quanzhou in the Yuan Dynasty, and during Emperor Hongwu's reign (1368–1398) of the Ming Dynasty, moved to Baiqi from Fashi. Their genealogy also records the relationship between them and Islam.

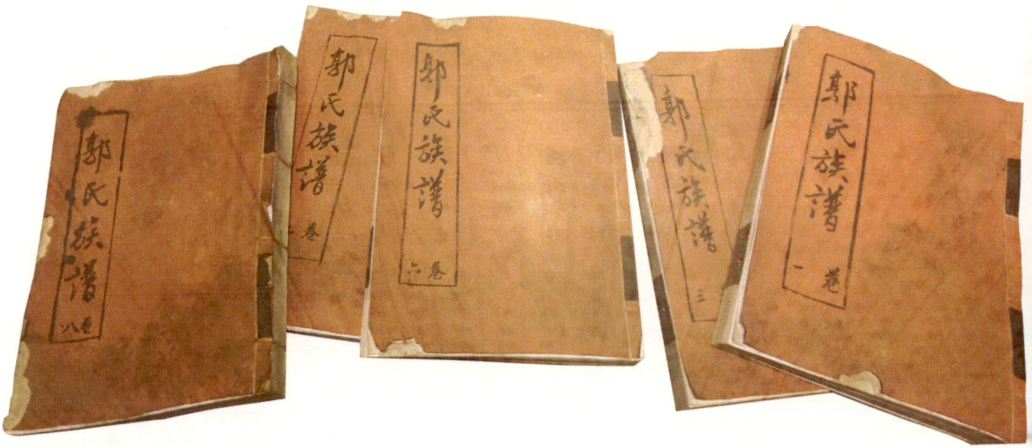

⊙ *The Guo Genealogy*, sample page

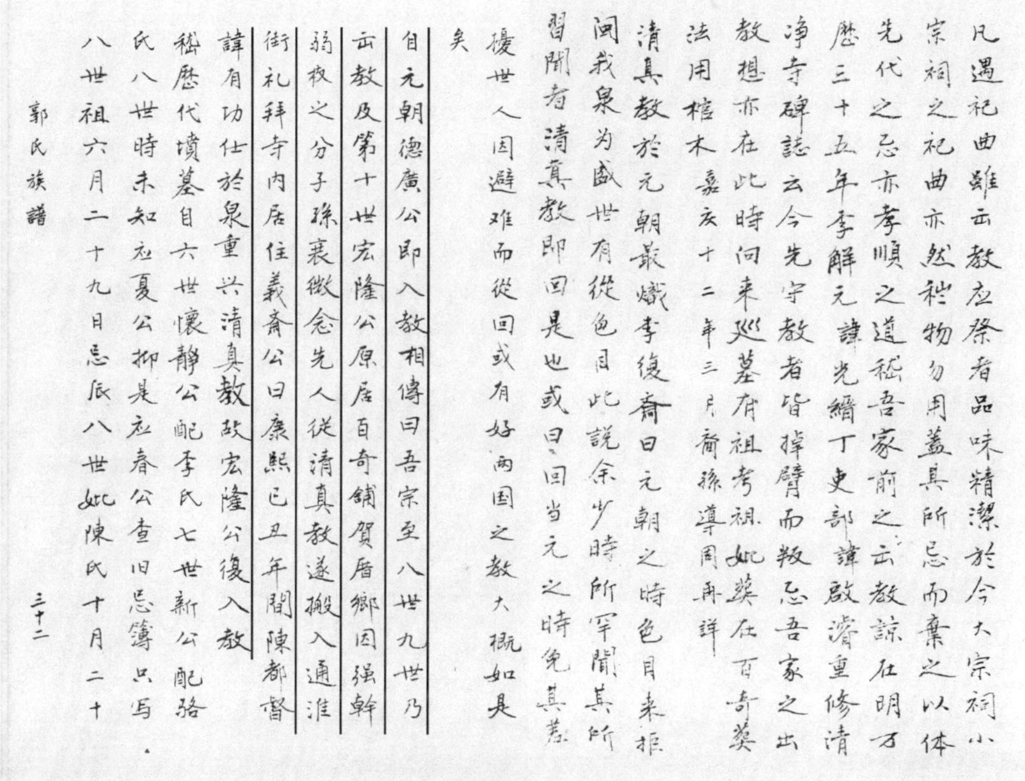
凡遇祀典雖回教應祭者品味精潔於今大宗祠小
宗祠之祀典亦然牲物勿用蓋其所忌而棄之以体
先代之忌亦孝順之道秘吾家前之回教諒在明万
歷三十五年李解元諱光縉丁吏部諱啟濬重修清
淨寺碑誌云今先守教者皆捧臂而教忌吾家之出
教想亦在此時向來巡墓府祖考祖妣葬在百奇葬
法用棺木嘉慶十二年三月裔孫導周再詳
清真教於元朝最熾李復齋曰元朝之時色目來拒
閩我泉為盛世有從色目此說余少時所罕聞其所
習聞者清真教即回是也或曰回当元之時免其惹
擾世人因避難而從回或有好兩国之教大概如是
矣
自元朝德廣公即入教相傳曰吾宗至八世九世乃
回教及第十世宏隆公原居百奇舖賀厝鄉因強幹
弱枝之分子孫衰微念先人從清真教遂搬入通淮
街礼拜寺内居住義齋公曰康熙己丑年間陳都督
諱有功仕於泉重興清真教故宏隆公復入教
稽歷代墳墓自六世懷靜公配李氏七世新公配駱
氏八世時未知應夏公抑是應春公查旧忌簿只写
八世祖六月二十九日忌辰八世妣陳氏十月二十
郭氏族譜 三十二

⦿ Record of Guo's family and Islam in *The Guo Genealogy*

Since the Ming Dynasty, the Guo family has made a living in the sea. They sailed and fished. Their old ferries and docks have survived to this day. And the descendants of the Guo family also adhered to the family motto, nurturing both brain and physique, and with their talent standing out in large numbers.

⊙ Baiqi Ancient Ferry

⊙ Shipping dock

Baiqi Township has a grand ancestral hall, the Guo Family Temple. Allegedly, it was built in 1432 and has been rebuilt many times. And the couplets, inscriptions, and plaques in the family temple demonstrate the relationship between the Guo family and the Arab region and their family beliefs.

⊙ The Guo Family Temple in Baiqi, Hui'an

⊙ Couplet at the gate of the Guo Family Temple

⊙ Couplets carved inside the temple

⦿ Reconstruction of Guo Family Temple in Baiqi

⦿ Xuanwei Hall of the Guo Family Temple in Baiqi, Hui'an

⦿ Memorial tablets of the Guo Family

⦿ The Guo Family's ancestral worship ritual

In Daishang Village, there is also a Guo ancestral hall. This traditional Hokkien-style ancestral hall contains many Islamic cultural elements.

⦿ (ABOVE) Ancestral Hall of the Guo Family

⦿ (LEFT) Pillars with Arabic texts on both sides of the gate of the ancestral hall of the Guo family

⦿ Lintels on both sides of the ancestral hall of the Guo family

⦿ The main hall of the ancestral hall of the Guo family

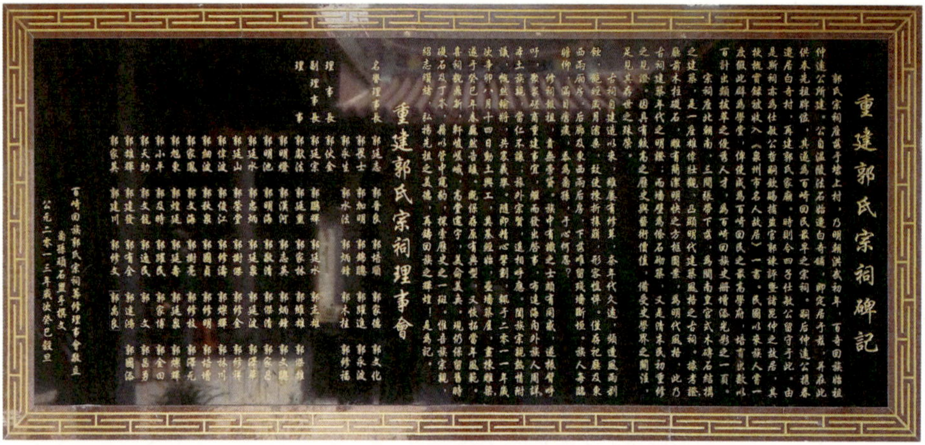

⦿ Stele of reconstruction of the ancestral hall of the Guo family stele

There are also many public halls in Baiqi Township, like the Dinghucuo Hall, which are used as venues for small-scale worship. The traditional Hokkien buildings preserved in Baiqi Township retain more or less traces of Islamic culture.

⦿ Dinghucuo Hall

The tombs of the Guo family are scattered in different locations, but they all adopt the form of a combination of Islamic altar-type tombs and Han-style tomb enclosures.

⦿ Tombs of Guo Zhongyuan and his wife

⦿ Close-up view of Guo Shichu's tomb

⦿ Panorama of Guo Shichu's Tomb

⦿ A couplet of Guo Shichu's tomb

⦿ Pavilion of Guo Shichu's Tomb

⦿ Shiyuan Cemetery

⊙ Tombs of Guo Tie and Guo Qi

⊙ Tomb of Guo Yizhai and his wife

Since the Guo family came to Fujian, they have coexisted harmoniously with the surrounding Han Chinese and learned their culture in Quanzhou.

⦿ Baiqi Nanyin music association

⦿ Inscription on the Completion of the New Site of Baiqi Nanyin music association

⦿ Nanyin music instrument

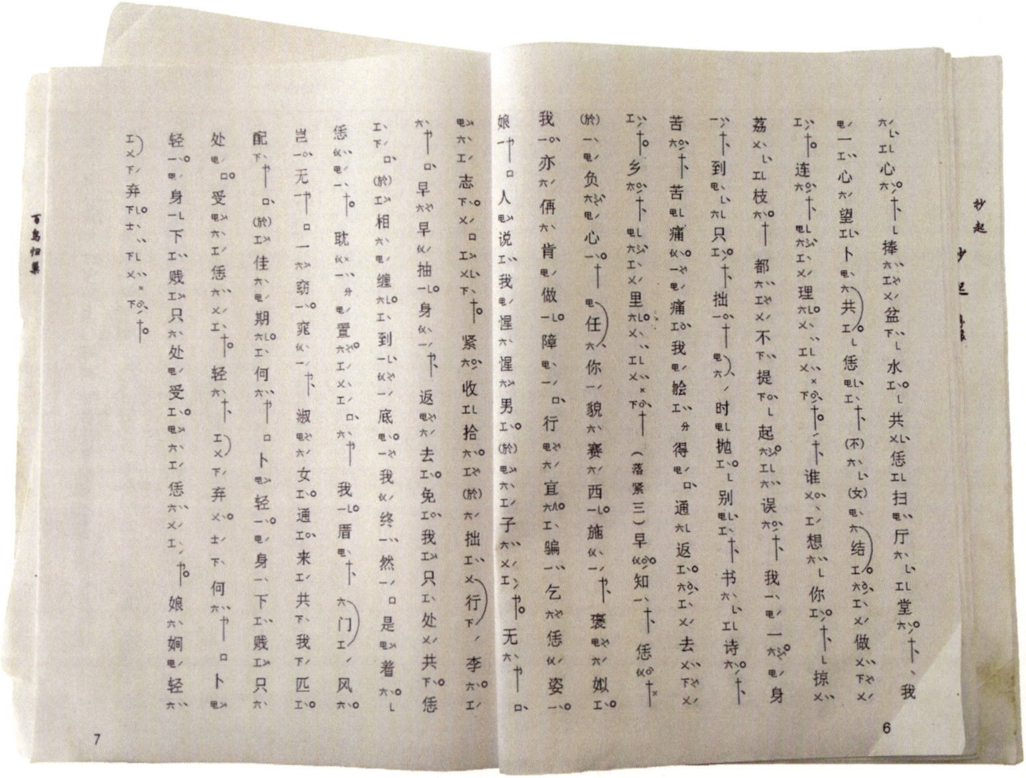

⦿ Nanyin music score

⦿ Nanyin rehearsal venue

⦿ Nanyin bandstand

In history, in addition to fishery production, maritime commerce, and trade, the Guo family also had military *juren* like Guo Bacui.

Guo Bacui, outstanding in martial arts, witty, courageous, and decisive, attended the imperial exam in the year of Gengzi (1780), ranked top of all students, and was named cavalry captain in 1780. In 1783, he was appointed company commander of the Xiamen Garrison. In 1785, he passed the examination and was promoted to the battalion commander of the Anping Garrison in Taiwan. In the first month of 1787, Lin Shuangwen of Taiwan led an army to besiege Zhuluo County. Guo was ordered to lead soldiers to rescue. He was hit by artillery and died at the age of 30. On the stone wall in the east side of the colonnade of the Holy Islamic Tombs, there is a monument that records Guo Bacui's renovation of part of the Holy Islamic Tombs in 1783.

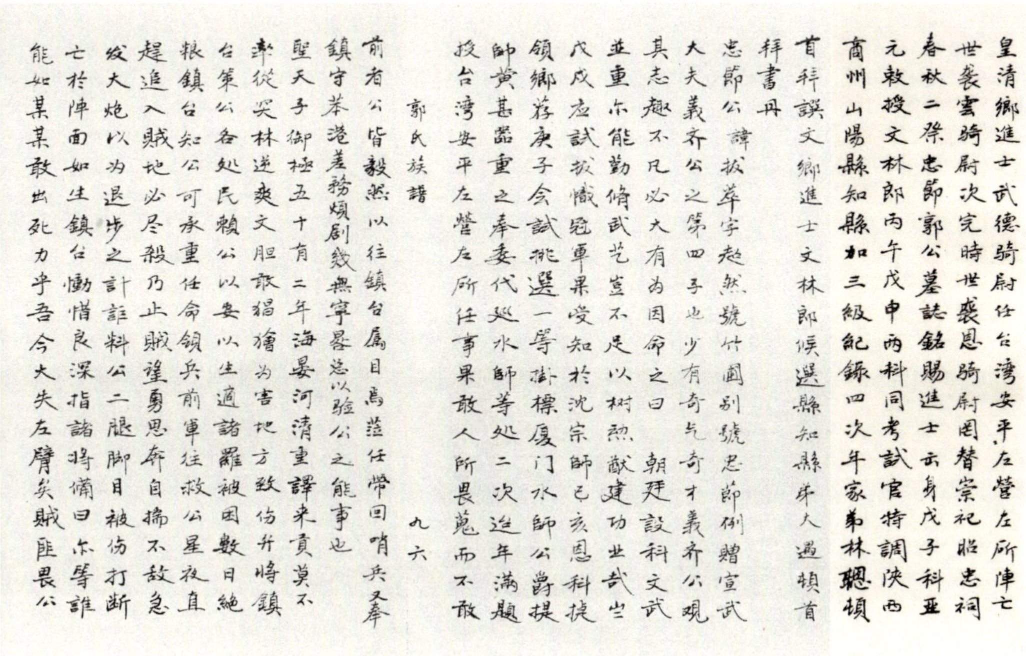

皇清鄉進士武德騎尉任台灣安平左營左所陣亡
世襲雲騎尉次完時世襲恩騎尉罔替崇祀昭忠祠
春秋二祭忠節郭公墓誌銘賜進士出身戊子科亞
元敕授文林郎丙午戊申丙科同考試官特調陝西
商州山陽縣知縣加三級紀錄四次年家弟林聰頓
首拜譔文鄉進士文林郎候選縣知縣弟人遇頓首
拜書丹
忠節公諱拔萃字超然號竹園別號忠節例贈宣武
大夫義齐公之第四子也少有奇氣奇才義齐公觀
其志趣不凡必大有為因命之曰朝廷設科文武
並重尔能勤脩武藝豈不足以樹勲獻建功業武[illegible]
戊戌應試拔幟冠軍果受知於沈宗師己亥恩科捷
領鄉薦庚子會試挑選一等掛標廈門水師公爵提
師黃甚器重之奉委代延水師等處二次迨年滿題
授台灣安平左營左所任事果敢人所畏葸而不敢

郭氏族譜

九六

前有公皆毅然以往鎮台屬目焉蓋任帶回哨兵又奉
鎮守茅港差務煩劇幾無寧晷是以驗公之能事也
聖天子御極五十有二年海晏河清重譯來貢莫不
率從獎林逆爽文胆敢猖獗為害地方致傷弁將鎮
台策公各処民賴公以安以生適諸羅被困數日絕
粮鎮台知公可承重任命領兵前軍往救公星夜直
趕追入賊地必尽殺乃止賊望勇思奔自掃不敢急
放大炮以為退步之計詎料公二腿脚目被傷打斷
亡於陣面如生鎮台慟惜良深指諸將備曰尔等誰
能如某某敢出死力乎吾今大失左臂矣賊匪畏公

⦿ Guo Bacui's epitaph in *Genealogy of the Guos*

⦿ Guarding stele beside the Jieguan Pavilion

CHAPTER 5

Cultural Integration—The Cultural Exchanges between Fujian, Persia, and Arabs

Fujian established close contact with Persia and the Arab world through the Maritime Silk Road. From the traditions of basic necessities of life that are preserved in Fujian and the Arab region, we cannot only find the traces of cultural exchanges between the two sides but also truly feel the breath of culture, which is precisely the most vital and exciting part of their cultural integration.

1 Incense: Across the Ocean

The exchanges between Fujian and the Arab world date back over a thousand years. Today, there are still products and cultures from Persia and the Arab world to be found in Fujian. The commodities sold to China by Arab and Persian merchants mainly include rare and precious treasures, incense, fabrics, and sundry goods, among which aromatic drugs were sold in bulk.

According to *A Description of Barbarian Nations*, *Records of Foreign People*, and *A Brief Account of Island Barbarians*, from the Song and Yuan Dynasties, many animals, plants, spices, and medicines were shipped to Fujian by Arab and Persian merchants, which made the use of incense in daily life widespread in Quanzhou.

⊙ Assorted spices

Frankincense, also known as olibanum, similar to turpentine, is the condensed particles of the natural secretion of trees. Frankincense was introduced to China as early as the Han Dynasty and to Fujian during the Min Kingdom period. There are records of it in *The New History of the Five Dynasties* and *A Description of Barbarian Nations, Records of Foreign People.*

Frankincense can be used externally to invigorate blood circulation and internally to reduce inflammation, help digestion, and relieve pain. It is described in the *Supplements of Materia Medica* by Chen Zangqi in the Tang Dynasty. Frankincense is also widely used in religious rituals, funerals, and people's daily celebrations.

⦿ (LEFT) Resin oozing from the bark of frankincense

⦿ (BELOW) Lentisk

◉ Coagulated granules of frankincense

◉ Frankincense

◉ Frankincense salvaged from a Song Dynasty ship in Quanzhou Bay

Jiangzhenxiang (lakawood), also known as jiangzhen, jiangxiang, jiguxiang, and zitengxiang, is the dried heartwood of the trunk and root of the leguminous plant lakawood. It was once a tribute to China by ancient foreign countries. And it was recorded in *Hai Yao Ben Cao* by Li Xun of the Five Dynasties.

Jiangzhenxiang has pain relief, hemostasis, antibacterial, and anti-inflammatory functions, which are detailed in the *Compendium of Materia Medica*. It is also written in *A Description of Barbarian Nations, Records of Foreign People* that Quanzhou locals widely used Jiangzhenxiang in the Song Dynasty.

⊙ Jiangzhenxiang plant

⊙ Jiangzhenxiang flowers

⊙ Jiangzhenxiang wood

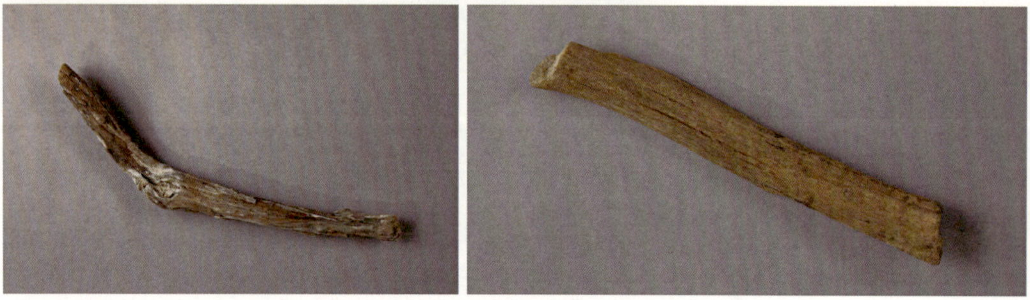

⊙ Jiangzhenxiang unearthed from a Song Dynasty ship in Quanzhou Bay

Styrax, also known as storax, was introduced to the Chang'an court in the name of "incense of soul" during the Yuanfeng Era (110–105 BC) of the Western Han Dynasty from present-day Syria, Ethiopia, and Yemen. It was recorded in Su Song's *Illustrated Materia Medica* in the Song Dynasty. And the styrax oil is mainly produced in Baghdad, Ghazni, Berbera, Maliba, and Daqin. It is written in *A Description of Barbarian Nations, Records of Foreign People* that styrax oil can be used for medical purposes.

⦿ Styrax plant

⦿ Styrax

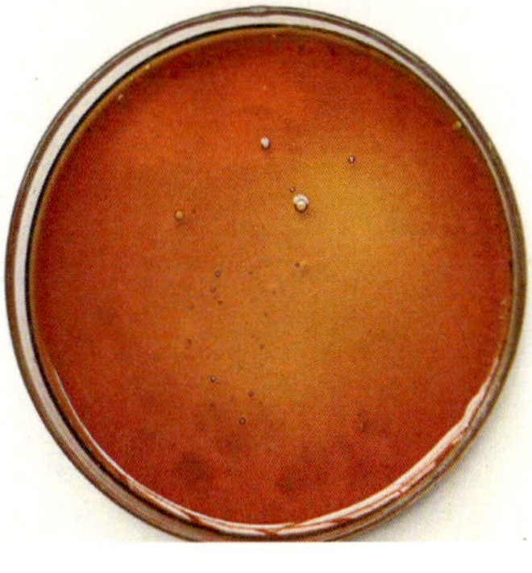

⦿ Styrax oil

Pepper, as an essential condiment, is nicknamed "black gold" and was once one of the important spices that promoted the Age of Discovery. It is divided into black pepper and white pepper. Black pepper is the sun-dried ear of the plant when its fruit begins to turn red; white pepper is the sun-dried ear of the plant when the fruit turns entirely red, which is soaked in water for several days, and whose outer skin is removed.

Pepper is hot in nature, tastes pungent, and can warm the middle, smooth the *qi*, eliminate phlegm, and detoxify, thus strengthening the stomach, helping digestion, and dispelling cold. It mainly treats cold phlegm, indigestion, abdominal pain, nausea, vomiting, diarrhea, cold dysentery, and other symptoms.

◉ Pepper plant

◉ Red pepper

◉ Green pepper

⊙ Black pepper

⊙ White pepper

⊙ Pepper unearthed from Song Dynasty ship in Quanzhou Bay

Betel nut, also known as areca-nut, has a pit like an olive, a spicy taste, and can be used as medicine. As early as the Jin Dynasty, the shape of the betel nut palm and how to eat the betel nut were described in *The Shape of Plants* and *Trees in the South*.

Betel nut tastes bitter and pungent, is warm in nature, and has the functions of helping to digest, resolving phlegm, treating malaria, killing parasites, diuretic, strengthening teeth, etc. It can treat parasitic accumulation, indigestion, abdominal distension and pain, diarrhea, malaria, edema, beriberi, phlegm, and other symptoms.

⦿ Betel nut palm

⦿ (ABOVE) Fruits on betel nut palm

⦿ (RIGHT) Betel nuts unearthed from a Song Dynasty ship in Quanzhou Bay

Ambergris, also known as ambergrease, is the dried product of sperm whale intestinal secretions. Newly discharged into the sea, the ambergris is a light black opaque waxy gelatinous lump at first, or dark brown like amber, which gradually hardens, fades, and emits an aroma after years of processing by sunlight, air, and seawater. Its color will also lighten and finally become white. Ambergris is crisp and light, chews like wax, sticks to the teeth, smells slightly fishy, and tastes sweet and sour. As a medicine, it promotes blood circulation, benefits the essence, nourishes the yang, and smoothes the blood vessels. It is mainly used to treat symptoms such as dizziness and dyspnea, pain in the heart and abdomen, indigestion, cough, asthma, etc.

⦿ Ambergris collected in the Forbidden City

⦿ Ambergris

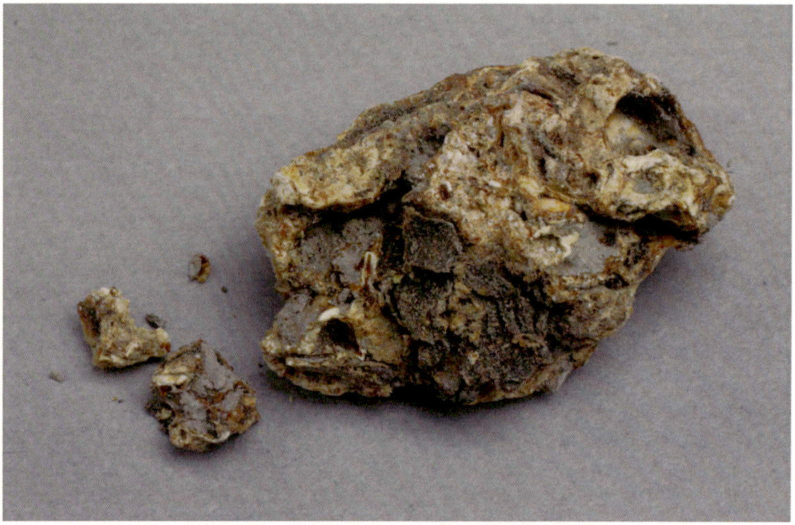

⊙ Ambergris unearthed from a Song Dynasty ship in Quanzhou Bay

⊙ Cinnamon for sale at an Arabian market

Foreign incense has changed the life structure and lifestyle of the Chinese people. It can be used as both a medicinal material and aromatherapy product. As people's understanding of incense has deepened, many kinds of incense have also been introduced into food processing, gradually changing people's original dietary structure.

Certainly, the exchange of spices and medicines was mutual. Local Chinese medicinal materials such as cinnamon, musk, Chinese rhubarb, and so on were also exported to Southeast Asia, Europe, and the Arab region via Arab merchants. The spread of traditional Chinese medicine in the Middle Ages greatly promoted trade and friendly exchanges between China, Persia, and the Arab world. This is not only an essential part of the history of exchanges on the Maritime Silk Road but also valuable evidence that Chinese spices and medicine have also made contributions to the development and enrichment of world medicine.

⊙ Cinnamon

⊙ Cinnamon powder

⦿ Chinese rhubarb plant

⦿ Chinese rhubarb seeds

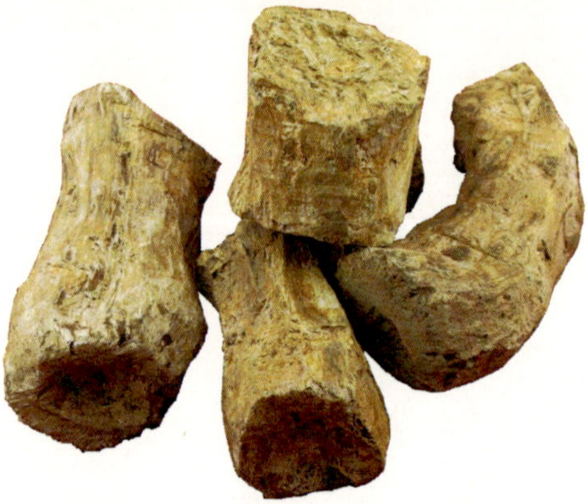

⦿ Chinese rhubarb stems

2 Flowers: Exotic Blossoms in Fujian

Historically, the flowers introduced into Fujian from Persia, and the Arab world mainly include *jasminum grandiflorum*, aloe, Jasminum sambac, henna, narcissus, etc.

Jasminum grandiflorum, also known variously as the Spanish jasmine, Royal jasmine, and Catalan jasmine, is native to Daqin. It was also cultivated in Persia and introduced to Byzantine Empire and the Western Regions first, then to southern China in the Han Dynasty. Its flowers are primarily white and highly aromatic. It has a mild nature, a slightly bitter taste, and the functions of soothing the liver and relieving depression, promoting *qi*, and alleviating pain. In addition, it is one of the primary raw materials of ancient perfumes. Ancient Fujianese women used to use it to adorn their headwear. Also, because of the prosperous foreign trade in the Song Dynasty, *Jasminum grandiflorum* was spread to Jiangsu, Zhejiang, and Northeast China through Fujian, making it a favorite garden plant.

⊙ White *Jasminum grandiflorum*

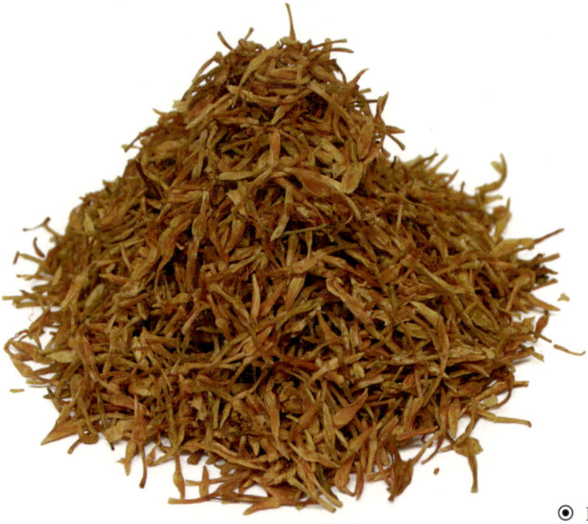

⦿ Dried *Jasminum grandiflorum*

⦿ Yellow *Jasminum grandiflorum*

Aloe, also known as Alua and Alwa, was introduced into China during the Eastern Han Dynasty. Because aloe is easy to grow and an ornamental plant with flowers and leaves, it gained wide popularity. It was planted in Fujian as early as the Song Dynasty.

Aloe has a bitter taste and is cold in nature. It is mainly used to treat diarrhea, purge intense liver heat, kill parasites and improve malnutrition. It works well on heat concentration, constipation, epilepsy, seizure, and child malnutrition. With specific curative effects on rough skin, facial wrinkles, scars, freckles, and acne, it is a natural medicine for skin care, hair care, and skin diseases. Traditional Chinese medicine also uses the lumps obtained through concentrating and drying the leaf juice as medicine for antisepsis. Aloe vera gel also has a specific antipruritic effect on mosquito bites, making it a plant that integrates edible, medicinal, cosmetic, and ornamental purposes.

⦿ Aloe flower

Jasminum sambac, also known as Arabian jasmine or Sambac jasmine, is native to the Western Regions and also cultivated in China. It was introduced to the South China Sea, the Lingnan area, via the Maritime Silk Road before the early Tang Dynasty and spread from Lingnan to Fujian during the Five Dynasties. It was quite popular in southern Quanzhou and northern Zhangzhou regions, recorded in *The History of Jasmine in Fujian and Guangdong* by Zhang Bangji.

Jasmine sambac has the functions of regulating *qi* and alleviating depression, dispelling filth, and harmonizing the middle. It has antibacterial, anti-inflammatory, and detoxifying effects on dysentery, abdominal pain, conjunctivitis, and soreness. Regularly drinking jasmine tea can remove liver heat and improve eyesight, help produce saliva and slake thirst, eliminate phlegm and treat dysentery, relax the bowels and alleviate water retention, clear wind-damp and relieve external symptoms, strengthen teeth and heart, consolidate *qi*, lower blood pressure and resist senility.

⦿ *Jasmine sambac*

⦿ Dried *jasmine sambac*

Henna is called the phoenix flower in Chinese because it resembles the tail of a phoenix. It originated in Persia and was introduced to China in the Tang Dynasty. It was mentioned *Bei Hu Lu* by Duan Gonglu. In the Song Dynasty, when many Arab merchants traveled to Quanzhou for business, they brought this plant to Quanzhou.

The unique natural plant pigments of henna and its strong inhibitory effect on fungi enable it to dye fingernails and treat onychomycosis and paronychia naturally. Freshly smashed henna, when applied externally, can treat soreness, furuncle, swelling and pain, and poisonous insect bites. And henna seeds are an antidote that can stimulate the menstrual flow, expedite childbirth, eliminate phlegm, and disperse accumulation lumps.

⦿ Red henna

⦿ Pink henna

⦿ White henna

Narcissus, also known as daffodil and jonquil, originated in the Persian Gulf region and was introduced to China in the Tang Dynasty. It has been cultivated for over a thousand years, as described in *The Miscellaneous Morsels from Youyang* by Duan Chengshi.

Because the bulbs of narcissus are similar to onions and garlic, it was called *yasuan* (garlic) in the Six Dynasties, and the Song people called it *tiancong* (onion). Since it came into China, scholars have widely loved it as it is slim and graceful, pure and clean, elegant and fragrant, becoming one of the main themes of traditional Chinese painting.

The narcissus in Chongming District of Shanghai and Zhangzhou of Fujian is the most famous in China. Widely planted in Zhangzhou and other southern Fujian regions, narcissus receives exquisite "carving" from local florists. The narcissus presents a richer shape and posture by removing the bulb and twisting and bending the leaves and branches.

⊙ Narcissus

The introduction of these flowers has enriched the variety of native Fujianese plants. People used them not only for the ornament of the living room but also for the decoration and dying of headwear or limbs. In addition, they have greatly inspired scholars to compose poetry. Many poems and chapters were written to sing their praises, and they have also become a popular theme for painters. Some flowers have also been used as medicinal materials due to their medicinal properties, thus completing the localization of exotic plants.

3 Treasures: Tribute to China

Historical documents such as *The History of the Song Dynasty, Biography of Foreign Countries, A Description of Barbarian Nations, Records of Foreign People*, and *Annotation of Representative Answers from the Region beyond the Mountains* record that in ancient times, rare treasures introduced into Fujian by Arab and Persian merchants included ivory, rhino horns, tortoiseshells, coral, etc.

For ivory, the incisor of the elephant's upper palate, the best is fine-textured and shiny. In the past, it was mostly carved into ornaments or art objects. In nature, there are Asian and African elephants.

The sources of ivory include natural teething, natural death, and the hunting of elephants by humans. The intact ivory brought by Arab merchants was for tributes or for raw materials in making art objects, while the cut pieces were used as medicine. They are cold in nature, sweet in taste, and have the functions of removing liver heat and calming the nerves, detoxifying, and strengthening muscles. And they can treat epilepsy, palpitation, phlegm-heat, carbuncles, and soreness.

⦿ Ivory products

⦿ Ivory

Rhino horns are divided into Asian rhino horns and African rhino horns. African rhino horns are mainly obtained from the local African black and white rhinos. In Arab countries, the rhino horn is regarded as a symbol of social status.

There are also two ways to obtain rhino horns: natural shedding and hunting by humans, which are described in *A Description of Barbarian Nations, Records of Foreign People*. Rhino horns are of great rarity, so rhino horn products have become one of the symbols of the ancient hierarchy. Sculptors turned the rhino horns into various cups, rafts, and so on according to their shapes.

Rhino horns also have the effects of removing body heat and cooling blood, calming the nerve and detoxifying, purging the liver heat, and cooling the heart. They can cure typhoid fever, panic attacks, mania, delirium, carbuncles, and pyogenic infections.

⦿ Rhino horn

⦿ A Mid-Qing Dynasty rhino horn cup carved with sea beasts

⦿ 17th–18th century rhino horn cup carved with celestial immortals offering birthday congratulations

⦿ A rhino horn cup carved with lotus and insect made between the Kangxi period (AD 1661–1722) and Yongzheng period (AD 1709–1722) in the Qing Dynasty

The Hawksbill sea turtle, also known as *Eretmochelys imbricata*, belongs to the family Cheloniidae and mainly lives in tropical and subtropical waters such as the Indian, Pacific, and Atlantic Oceans.

Tortoiseshell, as an imported good, refers specifically to the carapace of the Hawksbill sea turtle. It is a kind of organic gemstone. And it is widely popular for its colorful patterns, slightly transparent to translucent texture, and waxy to oily luster. People nickname it sea gold. It can be used as a raw material for jewelry such as bracelets and hairpins and to make combs, fans, boxes, and picks for musical stringed instruments like the *zheng*, *yijia*, *pipa*, etc.

As tortoiseshell is only available in the deep sea, the difficulty in obtaining it makes it a valuable medicinal material. It is cold in nature and sweet and salty. It has the effects of clearing heat, detoxifying and relieving convulsion. It can be used to treat fever, delirium, epilepsy in children, ulcers, carbuncle, and pyogenic infections, as recorded in the *Compendium of Materia Medica*.

⊙ Tortoiseshell bracelet

⊙ Qing Dynasty tortoiseshell bracelet with gemstones

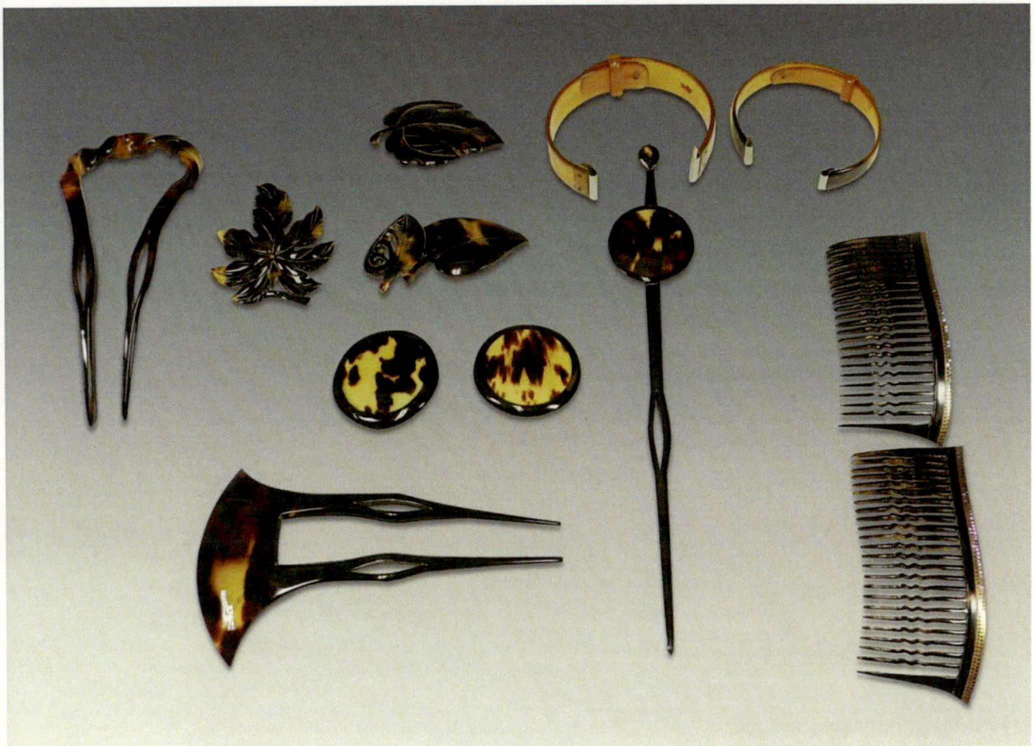

⊙ Twelve pieces of tortoiseshell accessories in the Qing Dynasty

⦿ Tortoiseshell treasure chest

⦿ Tiger-spot tortoiseshell cup

⦿ The tortoiseshell unearthed from the Song Dynasty ship in Quanzhou Bay

Coral, a submarine coelenterate, mainly grows in the equator and its nearby tropical and subtropical waters, where the annual average temperature is above 20°C. It is as hard as porcelain, not easy to break, and can be used as a medicinal material and as an ornament. As recorded in *Zheng Lei Materia Medica* and *A Description of Barbarian Nations, Records of Foreign People*, it was known as "red gold," produced in ancient times in the Mediterranean Sea, the Red Sea, and the Persian Gulf.

Coral improves eyesight, calms the nerves, relieves convulsions, and can treat symptoms such as dizziness, comas, internal heat, and persistent vomiting. Ancient navigators also believed wearing red coral could prevent lightning and hurricanes, calm the wind, and keep the voyage safe.

⦿ Coral

⦿ Red coral

As for pearls, also known as a shelled mollusk gem, Bahrain Island in the Persian Gulf and Marijukudi Port in the Gulf of Mannar, Sri Lanka, were pearl production centers in ancient times. Hepu of Guangxi Province, China, was also an important area of pearl production, as recorded in *A Description of Barbarian Nations, Records of Foreign People*. At the time, to avoid the tariffs of the bureau for foreign shipping, foreign merchants hid the pearls in their jackets and the handles of their umbrellas.

In a sequel to *Kui Xin Za Shi* by Zhou Mi of the Southern Song Dynasty, it is written that at that time a Muslim businessman named Pu Folian in Quanzhou possessed many pearls, reflecting the prosperity of foreign trade in Quanzhou.

⊙ Pearls

⊙ Pearl gold accessory unearthed from Li Jingxun's Tomb in Sui Dynasty

Colored glaze, also known as *liuli*, first appeared in Mesopotamia and then began to be produced in Egypt and was introduced to China, as mentioned in the excavations in Fuzhou.

These Arab treasures introduced into China enriched Chinese people's understanding and imagination of foreign countries at that time and also expanded the extension of traditional handicraft production. And many of them have inspired Chinese artisans to make more exquisite artworks.

⊙ Colored glaze ware unearthed in a Kang Tomb of Southern Han Dynasty

⊙ Arabian colored glaze

4 Etiquette and Customs: Daily Life and Festivals

In the Middle Ages, the cultures of ancient Persia, Arab and other regions were widely spread in Fujian. The people integrated and coexisted with the ancient Yue culture and the Central Plains culture, thus leading to the prosperity of Fujian's international trade, writing the legend of the Maritime Silk Road, and nurturing the inclusive and diverse Fujian culture.

The Islamic culture brought by Muslims differs significantly from Fujian culture. Its exotic customs, unique marriage customs, and burials have greatly enriched the local culture of Fujian, making Fujian in the Song and Yuan Dynasties colorful and charming.

As a traditional Muslim veil, the hijab was first used to distinguish noble women from enslaved women, who did not have to cover their faces. Since then, this tradition has been inherited by the Arabs, and various styles of hijab wrapping have evolved. In Quanzhou, women also commonly use the hijab (locally known as "foreign headscarves") to wrap their heads, which may be related to the legacy of the Islamic diaspora.

⦿ The prosperous Citong

⊙ Examples of hijab-wearing Muslim women

⊙ The custom of women in Quanzhou wearing "foreign headscarves"

Nanyin, a style of Chinese classical music in Quanzhou, is also known as the living fossil in the history of Chinese music. In *tē-sì-kóan* or the four lower instruments of Nanyin, the instruments retain the ancient traditions in terms of shape, composition, and performance. The *suona* horn and *pipa* used in Nanyin performance were introduced from Persia and Arabia.

⊙ *Suona* horn and Quanzhou ancient music score

⊙ The way the *pipa* is played in Arab regions

⊙ Photo of playing the *Nanyin Pipa*

⊙ Part of *The Night Revels of Han Xizai*

Arabic calligraphy, the art of writing Arabic script, holds a high social status in the Islamic world. After Arabic calligraphy was introduced into China, Chinese calligraphy was integrated into the creation of Arabic calligraphy. Finally, Arabic calligraphy with Chinese style was formed, including *jing zi hua*. And traditional Chinese framing forms, such as the central scroll, the vertically-hung scroll, the hand scroll, and couplets were adopted.

Arabic couplets can often be seen on the gates of local Muslim residences in Quanzhou. At the same time, there are also eye-catching Arabic house signs on the lintels. And the layout of the halls includes calligraphy tapestries, too. These are evidence of the integration of Chinese and foreign cultures.

⊙ Hall layout of a Muslim family in Quanzhou

⊙ (ABOVE) Arabic house signs for a Muslim family in Quanzhou

⊙ (RIGHT) An Arabic couplet on the gate of a Quanzhou Muslim residence

Today, festivals such as *Jumah, Eid al-Fitr,* and *Eid al-Adha* are still held in mosques throughout Fujian. Mosques in Quanzhou, Shaowu, Fuzhou, and Xiamen attract many domestic and foreign Muslims to visit.

Jumah is every Friday when Muslims go to the mosque to worship together. It is also a holiday stipulated by the Islamic prophet Muhammad after moving to Medina, and it has been used since then. On *Jumah*, local Muslims in Fujian and Muslim merchants from Egypt, Pakistan, and Kazakhstan, as well as Ningxia, Gansu, Xinjiang, and other places in northwestern China, will gather at the mosque for worship.

Eid al-Fitr is one of the three major religious festivals in Islam. Islam stipulates that Muslims start fasting on September 1st of the Islamic calendar, which should last one month. This period is also called *Ramadan*. According to the teachings, Muslims abstain from eating and drinking from before sunrise to after sunset every day during this month. The night of the twenty-seventh day of Ramadan is *Lailah al-Qadr*, and Quanzhou Muslims also call it Eve of Twenty-Eighth, which was as grand as the Han Chinese New Year's Eve. Each family holds a reunion banquet that night, entertaining families and friends with great delight.

On the last day of *Ramadan*, the imam climbs the moon observation deck to look for the new moon. If the new moon is seen, the fast stops the next day. The fast continues if no new moon is seen, but generally no more than three days. On the day of *Eid al-Fitr*, there is a ceremony and grand celebration, and Muslim women will get up early to prepare all kinds of exquisite food. All Muslims are dressed up after bathing that morning and go to the mosque to participate in the worship. In the mosque, Muslims, under the leadership of the imam, bow in the direction of the holy place of Mecca, the ancient mosque of Kaaba, and complete the prayer. In addition to the ceremonies mentioned above, they also sing and dance in accordance with national customs to celebrate.

On the day of *Eid al-Fitr*, the imam leads Muslims to the Holy Islamic Tomb of Lingshan after the worship rituals. Muslims first go to the tombs of the two disciples of Muhammad to worship them, sit on the ground, listen to the imam recite the Koran, and visit the graves of their ancestors or relatives to burn incense to mourn the deceased, paint the text on the old tombstones in red, and respectfully invite the imams to the grave to recite the scriptures and pray for the dead. This is the custom of sweeping the graves of Muslims in Quanzhou, called *youfen* in Chinese.

⊙ *Eid al-Fitr* Celebration at the Qingjing Mosque of Quanzhou

⦿ The Fuzhou Mosque celebrates *Eid al-Adha*

Eid al-Adha, also known as the Feast of the Sacrifice, is one of the three traditional Muslim festivals. It falls on December 10 of the Islamic calendar, the last day of the *Hajj*. On that day, Muslims should dress up and go to the mosque to attend the ceremony and greet each other. At the end of the ceremony, in addition to burning incense, those who are financially capable will also slaughter the cattle and sheep to celebrate. The meat of the slaughtered cattle and sheep should be divided into several portions and distributed to the imams, family, and friends. On this day, Muslims also have to go to the grave to commemorate their ancestors.

⦿ The Qingjing Mosque of Quanzhou celebrates *Eid al-Adha*

5 Architecture: Decorative Imprints in Fujian

Architecture is the embodiment of the individuality of a nation and civilization, and it also influences other culture's architecture during cultural interactions.

The style, layout, spatial arrangement, and ornaments of the Shaowu and Fuzhou mosques' main buildings broke through the original Arabic architectural paradigm. Based on integrating the local traditional wooden frame in Fujian, they have also absorbed the local hall structures, column layout, bucket arch system, roof shapes, and processing techniques.

⊙ Chinese-style Moon Pagoda of the Shaowu Mosque

⊙ Chinese roof of the Shaowu Mosque

⦿ (ABOVE) Hall structure of the Fuzhou Mosque

⦿ (RIGHT) *Dougong* (a system of brackets inserted between the top of a column and a crossbeam) of the main hall of the Fuzhou Mosque

⦿ Chinese roof of the main hall of the Fuzhou Mosque

We can also find the decorative openings of Arabic-style buildings in Fujian, including the processing technique of doors and windows with pointed arches, which is installed in local architecture. In Quanzhou, the exotic style of the Qingjing Mosque is widely appreciated by Quanzhou locals, and local architecture has absorbed this style, especially the shape of the pointed arch of the gate of the Qingjing Mosque.

⦿ Windows with pointed arch on Zhongshan Road, Quanzhou

⦿ Windows with pointed arch in Qilou of Quanzhou

Songkou Town, located in the southwest of Yongtai, Fujian Province, is the distribution center for commodities in the southwest of Yongtai. Among the many ancient dwellings in Songkou, there are many painted patterns with Arabian exoticism and ancient ships. These exquisite murals are concentrated on the water-shielding walls.

Xixiacuo is a large and well-preserved ancient residence in Dongpo Village. It consists of the main house and the two side houses. The carvings in the houses remain well preserved.

⦿ Entrance to Dongpo Village

⦿ Xixiacuo

⦿ Gate of Xixiacuo

⦿ Roof ornament of Xiaxiacuo

On the water-shielding wall under the left eaves of the main hall of Xixiacuo, there is a colorful mural depicting a port in the Arabian region. It presents a clear image of the Arab-style buildings, and in front of them are traditional Chinese multi-masted sailing ships. And the sail is a typical Chinese-style bamboo sail. Judging from the shape of the vessels, they must be traditional Fujian ships. As the sterns of the boats face the port building, this picture depicts the departure of Fujian merchant ships from a port in the Arabian region after the completion of trading.

There are also Arab-style architectural murals on the right water-shielding wall under the eaves. The most eye-catching in the mural is the minaret at the front. The Arabic buildings in the mural are obviously embedded with Chinese cultural elements. There are unrecognizable characters on the columns and lintels, whose pattern and style show their Chinese identity.

⊙ Xixiacuo mural of Arabic-style architecture and Chinese-style ships

⊙ Arabic murals in Xixiacuo

In Dongpo Village, Yonggengcuo is as famous as Xixiacuo. Locals also call it by the name Yongjincuo as Chen Yongjin built it during the reign of Emperor Qianlong (1735–1796) in the Qing Dynasty. It consists of three major parts of the main house, two side houses, and an eastern study.

⦿ Yonggengcuo

⦿ Gate of yonggengcuo

⦿ Courtyard of Yonggengcuo

⦿ Yonggengcuo mural of Arabic-style architecture and Chinese-style ships

There are Arabic-style painted patterns in the same spot of Yonggengcuo as in Xixiacuo. The mural on the water-shielding wall under the left eaves paints a row of Arabic-style buildings on the edge of the port, and there is a minaret inside the port wall. In the front of the mural are two three-masted Chinese ships with lion heads painted on the bows, and the sails were also made of bamboo. The ships were made in Fujian.

In the mural on the water-shielding wall under the right eaves, there is a two-story Arabic-style building, next to which is a minaret with a dome, giving off an exotic Arabian vibe.

Under the eaves of Yonggeng's house, there is also a mural painted with Arabic-style buildings.

⊙ Yonggengcuo murals of Arabic-style architecture

6 Porcelain: A Thousand Years of History at Sea

The firing of porcelain is an essential technological creation in ancient China, and Chinese porcelain is widely loved for its exquisite shape and excellent quality. The export of porcelain as a bulk commodity started in the Tang Dynasty, and since the Song and Yuan Dynasties, it has been continuously shipped to all parts of the world.

Fujian, known as the southeast mountain city, has become an important ceramic production and export base in southeast China because of its unique natural and geographical conditions.

In 2007, the ancient shipwreck *Nanhai One* from the Southern Song Dynasty was salvaged in the waters of Shangxiachuan Island, in Guangdong Province. The porcelain it carried is mainly from five major folk kilns, namely, the Fujian Dehua kiln, Fujian Cizao kiln, Fujian Minqingyi kiln, Jiangxi Jingdezhen kiln, and Zhejiang Longquan kiln.

⊙ Lifting the *Nanhai One* shipwreck caisson

⊙ Fujian porcelain on the *Nanhai One* shipwreck and remains of the ship's deck

⊙ Archaeological work at the excavation site of the *Nanhai One* shipwreck

⊙ The archaeological excavation site of the *Nanhai One* shipwreck

Gold accessories with noticeable exotic features were also unearthed with the porcelain. Judging from their production style and patterns, it is speculated that this Fujian Song Dynasty ship may have carried a certain number of Arab merchants and tourists at that time.

The kilneye (mouth of a kiln) and the style of the porcelain on Nanhai One exhibit distinct characteristics of export porcelain. It is a microcosm of the production at the kilns along the southeast coast of China in the Song Dynasty. These porcelains provided precious material evidence for studying overseas trade and the Maritime Silk Road in the Song Dynasty. At that time, the ancient ship likely sailed from the southeastern coast of China to Southeast Asia, India, or the Middle East for trade.

⊙ Porcelain and gilt belt from the *Nanhai One* shipwreck

⦿ Fujian Dehua kiln blue-white-glazed porcelain and Cizao kiln green-glazed porcelain scattered in the cabin of the *Nanhai One* shipwreck

⦿ Song Dynasty Cizao kiln porcelain from the *Nanhai One* shipwreck

⊙ Song Dynasty Cizao kiln porcelain inside the *Nanhai One* shipwreck

⊙ Song Dynasty Dehua kiln blue-and-white glazed kettle

⊙ Song Dynasty Dehua kiln porcelain set

⊙ Song Dynasty Dehua kiln blue-and-white glazed printed hexagonal kettle

⊙ Song Dynasty Dehua kiln blue-and-white glazed gourd vase

⊙ Song Dynasty Dehua kiln white glaze carved floral bowl

⊙ Gold ring

⊙ Gilt dragon-pattern ring

⊙ Gold necklace

Cizao kiln

The Cizao kilns, located in Cizao Town and adjacent areas in Jinjiang in Fujian Province, is a collective name for the remains of ancient kilns with common or similar historical and archaeological cultural connotations in and around Cizao Town. It has attracted the attention of relevant scholars since the 20th century. After extensive field investigations, archaeological excavations and specimen collections, 26 ancient kiln sites have been repeatedly discovered, including one kiln site of the Southern Dynasty, six of the Tang and Five Dynasties, 12 of the Song and Yuan Dynasties, and seven of Ming and Qing Dynasties. Most of these kiln sites are distributed on the hillsides on both sides of the Meixi River. Among the numerous sites of Cizao kilns, the Xikoushan kiln site of the Southern Dynasties, the Xiqianshan kiln site of the Tang and Five Dynasties, and Tuwei'an, Zhizhushan, Tongzishan, Jinjiaoyishan kiln sites of the Song and Yuan Dynasties are the most representative.

The Xikoushan kiln site resides on the hillside of Xikoushan, Xiaguanlu Village, in Cizao Town. This site dates back to the late Southern Dynasty. Archaeologically, only celadon wares were found there, including bowls, pots, cups, basins, and more.

⊙ Archaeologists from the Quanzhou Maritime Museum investigate the Xikoushan kiln site in Jinjiang

⊙ Archaeologists from the Quanzhou Maritime Museum inspect the Tuwei'an kiln site

The Tuwei'an kiln site sits on a small hillside on the south bank of Meixi River in Lingpan Village. The site area is about 30,000 square meters. The thickest part of its accumulation horizon is 4.5 meters. And most of the porcelains unearthed there are daily life utensils, including bowls, *junchi* (a kind of kettle), bottles, pots, kettles, jars, plates, basins, urns, flower pots, porcelain pillows, burners, incense burners, etc. And they are rich in shapes, which is rare in the kiln sites of the same period in Fujian, which suggests that the Tuwei'an kiln site was one of the most important kilns that made export porcelain at that time.

The Jinjiaoyishan kiln site is located in Jinjiaoyi Mountain, west of Qianpugoubian Village, Cizao Town, Jinjiang. The kiln site covers an area of about 40,000 square meters. It was founded in the late Tang and Five Dynasties and abandoned in the late Yuan Dynasty. It was one of the important kilns for export porcelain in Quanzhou and Fujian during the Song and Yuan Dynasties, as well as one of the better-preserved sites among the 12 Cizao kiln sites of the Song and Yuan Dynasties.

⦿ Jinjiaoyi Mountain of Jinjiang

⦿ Excavation site of the Jinjiaoyishan kiln site

⦿ Panorama of the Jinjiaoyishan kiln site

⦿ Old kilns of the Jinjiaoyishan kiln site

⦿ The Jinjiaoyishan kiln site is a national key cultural relics protection site

The Jinjiaoyishan kiln site, nearby clay excavation site, waterway, and Quanzhou Bay constitute the entire chain of ancient porcelain production and transportation for export. They comprehensively and systematically demonstrate the porcelain export process in ancient times and thus hold important academic value.

⊙ Song Dynasty Cizao kiln green glazed floral dish from the *Nanhai One* shipwreck

⊙ Song Dynasty Cizao Kiln brown glazed flat kettle

⊙ Song Dynasty Cizao kiln small-mouth bottle and brown glazed jar

⊙ The ancient well where the black glazed bowl on which is written *Ming Jiao Hui* (Ming Church) in the Song Dynasty was unearthed

In 1979, an ancient well was discovered 20 meters in front of the Jinjiang Thatched Hut, where a black glazed bowl on which was written *Ming Jiao Hui* (Ming church) and scores of fragments were unearthed. The bowl was black-glazed inside and semi-glazed outside. The inside of the bowl is inscribed with the characters *Ming Jiao Hui*. Among the scores of fragments unearthed, 13 are inscribed with Ming, Jiao, Hui, etc.

Archaeological investigations found that the *Ming Jiao Hui* bowl was fired from a Dashuwei kiln from the Cizao Kilns in the Song Dynasty. It is believed to be tableware specially made for the local believers of Manichaeism (a dualistic religious system with Christian, Gnostic, and pagan elements) in the Song Dynasty, making it an important symbol for the prosperity of Manichaeism in Quanzhou. This discovery also provided precious material data for studying Manichaeism activities in Quanzhou in the Song Dynasty. The bowl was labeled a national first-grade cultural relic because of its significant historical value and is now collected in the Jinjiang Museum.

The exterior of the Jinjiang Thatched Hut

Song Dynasty *Ming Jiao Hui* black glazed bowl, collected by the Jinjiang Museum

Statue of Mani

Dehua Kiln

The Dehua kilns a famous export porcelain production kiln system along the coast of Fujian. Dehua kilns are mainly distributed in Dehua County. As one of China's renowned porcelain industry centers, Dehua began firing primitive celadon as early as the Shang and Zhou Dynasties. It was fully developed during the Tang and Song Dynasties and entered its heyday in the Ming Dynasty. It is still an important porcelain industry base today.

Dehua kiln had long firing hours and various products, and the glaze color of porcelain varied in different periods. During the Song and Yuan Dynasties, blue-white glazed porcelain was the main product, and such porcelain included powder boxes, kettles, *junchi*, bowls, bottles, etc.

⦿ Song Dynasty Dehua kiln blue-and-white glazed bell-mouth bottle

⦿ (ABOVE) Song Dynasty Dehua kiln white-glazed four-ear jar from the *Nanhai One* shipwreck

⦿ (RIGHT) Song Dynasty Dehua kiln white-glazed bell-mouth bottle from the *Nanhai One* shipwreck

⊙ Song Dynasty Dehua kiln blue and white-glazed kettle from the *Nanhai One* shipwreck

⊙ Song Dehua kiln blue and white-glazed printed double-ear jar from the *Nanhai One* shipwreck

⊙ Song Dynasty Dehua kiln blue and white-glazed bowl from the *Nanhai One* shipwreck

⊙ Song Dynasty Dehua kiln white-glazed powder box from the *Nanhai One* shipwreck

⊙ Statue of Guanyin by He Chaozong of the Ming Dynasty, collected by the Quanzhou Maritime Museum

In the Ming Dynasty, Dehua kilns mainly produced white-glazed porcelain, whose quality was significantly improved compared with the previous generations. It was praised as "ivory white" and "Chinese white" for its smooth, bright glaze color and milky, cream-like appearance. The porcelain figures produced in this period are extremely exquisite, and all kinds of statues are incredibly vivid, especially the porcelain figures made by He Chaozong. The world is fascinated with his works. After the mid-Ming Dynasty, blue-and-white inscriptions appeared on a few white-glazed porcelains. In the Qing Dynasty, Dehua kilns mainly fired white-glazed, blue-and-white, and multi-colored porcelain.

The Qudougong Site of Dehua kiln system is located in Xunzhong Town, Dehua County. The site was built on a mountain, high in the north and low in the south. The production tools unearthed include impressions, blank-making turntables, iron knives for knocking saggars, saggar mats, various types of saggars, etc. (method of creating confined atmospheres within a container or saggar). Over ten kinds of utensils were unearthed, including bowls, plates, dishes, pots, jars, bottles, wash bowls, cups, boxes, and goblets, whose styles and patterns are rich, thus distinguishing it from other porcelain kilns. According to the assessment of archaeological experts, this kiln site is one of the most distinctive ancient kiln sites in Dehua in the Song and Yuan Dynasties.

⦿ Dehua Qudougong Kiln Site

⦿ Dragon Kiln of Dehua Qudougong Kiln Site

The Meiling Site of Dehua Kiln is located in Sibin Village, Sanban Town, Dehua County. At an altitude of over 400 meters, it covers an area of about 1.17 square kilometers, including three main areas of Neiban District, Dalongkou District, Meiling District, and a porcelain clay processing area on the flat ground by the stream at the mountain foot. This site dates back to the Song and Yuan Dynasties. There are many representative products of Dehua kilns, such as blue-and-white porcelain from the Song and Yuan Dynasties, white porcelain and blue-and-white porcelain from the Ming and Qing Dynasties.

⊙ Aerial view of the Meiling Site of the Dehua Kiln

⊙ The interior of the kilns in the Meiling district of the Dehua kiln site

⊙ Meiling District Kiln Branch Dehua Kiln Site

⊙ Saggars excavated at the Meiling site of Dehua kiln

Since the Song and Yuan Dynasties, as maritime trade continued to thrive while meeting local demand, Dehua kiln products were also exported to Japan, Southeast Asian countries, India, Africa, and Europe. In addition to the products, Dehua ceramics firing technology and kiln construction form were also spread overseas through the Maritime Silk Road and significantly impacted the development and progress of international porcelain production technology.

Having visited Quanzhou, the Italian traveler Marco Polo in the Yuan Dynasty praised that bowls and porcelains made in Dehua kiln were both beautiful, numerous, and of high quality but at a low price. "Many finished products are available in the city, and one Venetian silver coin can afford up to eight porcelain cups." Dehua porcelain was highly praised by people at home and abroad due to its great variety and high quality. It became an important export commodity on the ancient Maritime Silk Road and an important carrier of old foreign cultural exchanges.

⊙ Archaeological excavation site of a Song Dynasty white glazed four-ear jar made in the Dehua kiln from the *Nanhai One* shipwreck

Zhangzhou Kiln

Zhangzhou kiln is a general term for the kiln industry in Zhangzhou during the Ming and Qing Dynasties. Zhangzhou kilns were mainly distributed in Pinghe, Zhangpu, Nanjing, Yunxiao, Zhao'an, and Hua'an. Nansheng Kiln, Wuzhai Kiln of Pinghe County, and Dongxi kiln of Hua'an County were the most representative. During the Ming and Qing Dynasties, with the rise of the Moon Port in Zhangzhou, Zhangzhou kiln porcelain became an important export product, and rose to fame at home and abroad for its unique cultural and artistic charm.

Most of the porcelains produced by Zhangzhou kilns were blue-and-white. Still, there was also a small amount of white-glazed porcelain, blue-glazed porcelain, monochrome-glazed porcelain, and multicolored porcelain. Among them, blue-and-white porcelain and multicolored porcelain are also known as "Clark porcelain," "Cochin porcelain," and "South China three-color-glazed porcelain." According to a blue-and-white *Porcelain Appraisal* by Zhang Pusheng, there were two main sea transport routes for Clark porcelain in the Ming and Qing Dynasties: one was from the coastal ports of Fujian and Guangdong to Africa, and then past the Cape of Good Hope and along the west coast of Africa to Western European countries; the other was from ports in Zhangzhou, Fujian, Xiamen, first to Manila in the Philippines, and then across the Pacific Ocean eastward to the port of Acapulco in Mexico, where the Clark porcelain was transported to the port of Veracruz near Mexico City by land, from where it was shipped to Western European countries.

⦿ Ming Dynasty Zhangzhou Kiln multicolored plate

⦿ Ming Dynasty Zhangzhou Kiln plate with the eight-diagram pattern

⦿ Ming Dynasty Zhangzhou Kiln large blue-and-white plate with lotus pattern

⦿ Aerial view of Dongkoupogou Kiln site of the Nansheng kiln site

The Dongkoupogou Kiln of the Nansheng kiln site is a representative porcelain kiln site of the Zhangzhou kiln system. It is located in Wuzhai Township, Nansheng Town, Pinghe County. And its kilns are densely distributed on the hills of both sides of Huashan Creek, a tributary of Jiulong River and its small tributaries.

There are eight main remains of the Nansheng kiln, including the Huazailou kiln, Tiankeng kiln, Wuzhaidalong kiln, Huazailou kiln, Dongkoupogou kiln, Dalong kiln, Erlong kiln, and Tianzhongyang Kiln. These kilns started in the Song and Yuan Dynasties and peaked from the middle and late Ming Dynasty to the beginning of the Qing Dynasty. They rose and became a representative of export porcelain but gradually declined during the Kangxi period (1661–1722) of the Qing Dynasty.

Porcelain fired in the Nansheng kiln was an important foreign trade commodity for the Moon Port in the Ming Dynasty. The most representative types were blue-and-white porcelain, painted porcelain, and three-color-glazed porcelain. And most of them were large plates and boxes with rich ornamental patterns. There were also a few bottles, burners, jars, bowls, plates, dishes, cups, and other utensils.

The Nansheng Kiln represents the highest level of Zhangzhou's export porcelain industry in the 16th and 17th centuries. It is an important physical relic of the foreign trade of ceramics in the southeastern coastal areas of China during the Ming and Qing Dynasties. Its products were exported to Japan, Southeast Asia, Africa, and Europe.

◉ The remains of the Dongkoupogou Kiln site of the Nansheng kiln site

The remains of the Shangxiaxing kiln site

The kilns and saggar porcelain pieces piled up at the Shangxiaxing kiln site

Younger than the Nansheng kiln, the Dongxi kiln is another representative of Zhangzhou export porcelain kilns. It was built in the middle and late Ming Dynasty, reached its peak in the mid and late Qing Dynasty and lasted until the early Republic of China. Its kilns were mainly distributed in Hua'an and Nanjing. There were two types of kilns: ascending kiln and dragon kiln, and their representatives included the Shangxiaxing kiln site and the Fengmenkeng kiln site.

The Shangxiaxing kiln site stands at the foot of Shangxiaxingxi Mountain in Hua'an County, and an ascending kiln has been discovered, which dates back to the late Ming Dynasty. The unearthed cultural relics there include kiln tools and porcelain-making tools, such as saggars, bedders, porcelain molds, test pieces, as well as a significant number of porcelain fragments of daily products, which are mainly blue-and-white porcelain, and a few white porcelain, celadon, and brown-glazed porcelain.

⊙ Aerial view of the Shangxiaxing kiln site

⊙ Aerial view of the Fengmenkeng kiln site

The Fengmenkeng kiln site lies in Nanjing County, only a stream away from the Shangxiaxing kiln site. Most production there occurred from the late Ming Dynasty to the early Republic of China period. The products unearthed there have a wide variety of types and shapes, including primarily blue-and-white porcelain, white porcelain celadon, and a few brown-glazed porcelains.

In general, the products fired by the Dongxi kiln were mainly blue-and-white porcelain, as well as celadon, white porcelain, beige-glazed porcelain, brown-and-black glazed porcelain, blue-glazed porcelain, and multicolored porcelain; most of them were daily utensils, and their patterns include flowers, tangled chrysanthemums, landscapes, and fishing, etc. And they present new features in the appearance. Dongxi kiln products were exported to Japan, Southeast Asia, Africa, and Europe and found in many shipwrecks of the same period.

⦿ Remains of the Fengmenkeng kiln site of Dongxi kiln

⦿ Saggars at the Fengmenkeng kiln site of Dongxi kiln

In the middle and late Ming Dynasty, the production of Zhangzhou kiln porcelain became increasingly mature, so that it could be customized on a large scale as required by the clients. The orders from western countries increased significantly. And blue-and-white and multicolored porcelain plates were the most characteristic and representative products.

For example, the large blue-and-white plate with Arabic text below is a Zhangzhou kiln product from the late Ming Dynasty. The plate is huge, with three layers of decorative patterns of Arabic text inside, which appear calm, elegant, and smooth. It is a typical example of cultural exchanges between China and foreign countries.

⊙ Late Ming Dynasty Zhangzhou kiln large blue-and-white plate with Arabic texts

This Zhangzhou kiln multicolored plate with Arabic texts collected in the Palace Museum uses red and green colors to paint the Arabic texts, which sing the praise of Allah. It is specially customized for Muslims.

⊙ Late Ming Zhangzhou kiln multicolored plate with Arabic texts

Fujian kilns such as Cizao kiln, Dehua kiln, and Zhangzhou kiln also produced a peculiarly shaped and brightly colored water bottle called *junchi*. The so-called *junchi*, also known as a washing bottle, was originally a Buddhist utensil from India. It was a water bottle for wandering monks to wash their hands.

⊙ Song Dynasty Cizao kiln green-glazed *junchi* with double dragons playing with pearls

⊙ Song Dynasty Cizao kiln green-glazed *junchi*

⊙ Song Dynasty Cizao kiln green-glazed *junchi*

⊙ Song Dynasty Cizao kiln *junchi* with double dragons

⊙ Quanzhou Cizao kiln green-glazed *junchi*

With the spread of Buddhism, the *junchi* was introduced to Southeast Asian countries from India and was accepted by believers. Since the 8th century, as Arab merchants traveled eastwards, Islam began to spread into Southeast Asia and continued to develop. The *junchi* is mainly used to hold water for drinking and hand washing, which is in line with Islamic teachings, so it became accepted by Muslims as a portable utensil to store water for hand washing when praying on the journey.

After that, the *junchi* produced in Fujian was also transported to the Arab regions through Southeast Asia. In Islamic religious life, water is used on many occasions. Water is required for "*wugong*" before the Five Pillars of Islam every day and after three meals. Therefore, the *junchi* also became a commonly used utensil by Muslims.

Over the years, products from Cizao kilns, Dehua kilns, and Zhangzhou kilns have been unearthed in East Asia, Southeast Asia, South Asia, West Asia, East Africa, North Africa, etc. Their shapes and patterns reflect that Fujian porcelain met the demand of overseas markets. And the *junchi*, a famous water bottle overseas, which spans the two major religions of Buddhism and Islam, has also become typical material evidence of Fujian's Maritime Silk Road trade. In 1976, during the excavation of the Dehua kiln site in Qudougong, Dehua, 209 pieces of *junchi* were unearthed, which caused a sensation within the archaeological community.

⊙ Song Dynasty Dehua kiln blue-and-white glazed chrysanthemum-pattern *junchi*

⊙ Song Dynasty Dehua kiln blue-and-white glaze tangled-branch *junchi*

Ibn Battutah (1304–1377) of Morocco was a world-famous traveler and author of *The Travel Notes of Ibn Battutah*, in which he described the places he visited in Quanzhou, Hangzhou, and other destinations in China and recorded the export of Chinese silk and ceramics at the time.

⦿ *Research on The Travel Notes of Ibn Battutah: From Morocco to China*, Chinese translation, cover

⦿ Statue of Ibn Battutah

To commemorate the 50th anniversary of establishing diplomatic relations between the People's Republic of China and the Kingdom of Morocco, the two countries jointly issued three commemorative stamps and envelopes on November 1, 2008. The images on the three stamps are the ancient city gate of Morocco, the Great Wall, and two typical porcelain and traditional window lattices of the two countries, respectively. All stamps were printed with the national flags of China and Morocco and the number "50" and adopted the commemorative postmark of Dehua kiln *junchi*.

The 50th-anniversary silk-porcelain stamps to celebrate the establishment of diplomatic relations between the People's Republic of China and the Kingdom of Morocco are the first set of diplomatic stamps that combine the two elements of silk and porcelain. It embeds Dehua white porcelain *junchi* on silk, and its background image is the route map of Ibn Battutah to China, where a relief ship is riding the wind and waves in the blue sea.

⊙ The cover of the stamp album commemorating the 50th anniversary of the establishment of diplomatic relations between the People's Republic of China and the Kingdom of Morocco

⊙ Inside page of the commemorative stamp album of the 50th anniversary of the establishment of diplomatic relations between the People's Republic of China and the Kingdom of Morocco

⊙ Commemorative stamps with the Ancient City Gate of Morocco and the Great Wall of China

⊙ Commemorative stamps with typical porcelains from China and Morocco

⊙ Commemorative stamps with traditional window lattices of China and Morocco

Front of the commemorative envelop of the 50th anniversary of the establishment of diplomatic relations between China and Morocco

Back of the commemorative envelope of the 50th anniversary of the establishment of diplomatic relations between China and Morocco

The Full Stamps of the 50th Anniversary of the Establishment of Diplomatic Relations between the People's Republic of China and the Kingdom of Morocco

⊙ Malindi and Mombasa in Zheng He's Navigation Chart

⊙ The Vasco da Gama Tower in the ancient port of Malindi, Kenya, where Zheng He's fleet of voyages visited

Qalhat, the trading port site of Oman, was an important port from the Arabian Sea eastward to India, Southeast Asia, and China. In recent years, Oman and France have conducted joint investigations and excavations and discovered many Chinese ceramics, including products from Dehua kilns in the Yuan Dynasty.

In Kenya, Mombasa is one of the places where the most ancient Chinese porcelains are found. In 1405, Zheng He, a Chinese navigator of the Ming Dynasty, led a vast fleet and started the great pioneering seven voyages to the West. His fleet reached the farthest to Malindi (now Malindi, Kenya) and Mombasa (now the port of Mombasa, Kenya), south of the equator on the east coast of Africa.

⊙ Port Malindi, Kenya

⊙ Yuan Dynasty Dehua kiln dish fragment, unearthed in Qalhat, Oman

⦿ Mosque sites in Malindi

⦿ The tops or upper part of the tomb columns are decorated with Chinese porcelain

The village of Mambrui, 15 kilometers north of Malindi, is an ancient fishing village by the sea. Two cylindrical tombstones are standing in an overgrown cemetery, on which 10 Chinese porcelain plates used to be embedded, but only four remain.

In recent years, the Kenyan Archaeological Team of Peking University has also participated in the archaeological excavation of Mambrui, and found many Chinese porcelain pieces.

In the southeast corner of Mombasa Island, Kenya stands a magnificent architecture—Fort Jesus, which is over 100 meters long and 80 meters wide. On the north and west sides of the fort, there is a moat with a width of 3 meters to 12 meters and a depth of 13 meters, which separates the port from the land. The port's south and east sides face the sea. A barrier is carved out of natural coral rocks, making it easy to defend but difficult to attack the fort. Thus, it was used to guard the Port of Mombasa. Since the opening of the new route, Mombasa has become an important supply point and cargo distribution center on the new route to the East and Fort Jesus has become the spot that every country wanted to occupy.

⦿ Fort Jesus of Mombasa

⦿ Ancient Chinese Porcelain collected in Fort Jesus in Mombasa

⦿ Dragon urns collected in Fort Jesus in Mombasa

⦿ Door frame decorated with Chinese porcelain tiles on Lamu Island

Fort Jesus displays the various cultural relics discovered in its vicinity over the past decade. The most striking exhibits are the over 100 pieces of porcelain from China, including dragon urns from the Fujian Cizao Kilns. There are also blue-and-white porcelain pieces and Longquan kiln porcelain.

It is understood that some of them were excavated in the Fort, while others were found in Malindi, near Mombasa. These porcelains from the Ming and Qing dynasties show that China had indirect contact with Africa at least 600 years ago.

Lamu Island is a tropical island in northeastern Kenya in the Indian Ocean. As the oldest residential town in Kenya, Arabs began to settle on this island as early as the 9th century, so now it has a strong Islamic style. The locals believe that over 600 years ago when Zheng He came to Kenya, Lamu Island was the first place he landed. In residents' homes, Chinese porcelain can still be found from time to time. Now in the Lahm Museum, there are displays of Chinese porcelain over the centuries.

As an overseas bulk commodity along with silk and tea, Porcelain occupies a prominent position on the Maritime Silk Road. Its attributes make it easier to be preserved, so it has also become an important witness of maritime trade routes. It continues to occasionally be discovered during archaeological excavations in ports around the world, so some scholars call the Maritime Silk Road the Porcelain Road. In the process of exporting porcelain, there was a change in not only the way of life from where it was exported but also the production and firing process of where it was exported. For example, the customization orders have greatly enriched the shape and decoration of the porcelain and promoted the cultural exchanges between the East and the West.

Summary

Fujian was a vital window and channel for China's foreign exchanges, where different ethnic groups met and different civilizations interacted. The Arab and Persian historic relics preserved in Fuzhou, Quanzhou, Xiamen, and Shaowu, including mosques, inscriptions, and stone statues in different historical periods, are witnesses to the personnel exchanges and cultural integration between Fujian, Persia, and the Arab world, and also to the historical fact of Fujian is an essential point of the Maritime Silk Road.

The ocean connects the world. Ships and navigation techniques, which are important carriers of the marine society, were also exchanged between Fujian and Persian and Arabian merchants and sailors. Regarding the exchanges between Fujian and Persia and the Arab world in history, merchants, missionaries, envoys, and travelers were the promoters of their cultures. The exchange of products between the East and the West has influenced the diet and craftsmanship of the locals, the spread of exotic cultures has broadened people's horizons, and the reference of architectural styles and clothing styles has also satisfied the aesthetic needs of different groups of people. All these are remarkable footprints of the Chinese and foreign cultures.

Today, the tradition of cultural exchanges between Fujian and Arab countries continues. It is believed that under the Belt and Road Initiative, Fujian and Arab countries will have closer exchanges and continue to write new chapters of peaceful exchanges.

References

[Ming] Anonymous. *Two Sea Routes*. Annotated by Xiang Da. Zhonghua Book Company, 2012.

[Han] Ban, Gu. *The Book of Han*. Annotated by Yan, Shigu. Zhonghua Book Company, 1964.

[Moroccan] Battuta, Ibn. *Exotic Wonder— Travel Notes of Ibn Battuta (complete translation)*. Translated by Li Guangbin. Ocean Press, 2008.

Cai, Yaoping, Zhang Ming, and Wu Yuanpeng. *Academic Quanzhou*. Central Literature Publishing House, 2003.

Chen, Baoqiang. "Frankincense in the Song Dynasty Fragrance Trade." Master's thesis, Jinan University, 2000.

Chen, Dasheng. *Islamic Stone Carvings in Quanzhou*. Ningxia People's Publishing House, Fujian People's Publishing House, 1984.

Chen, Gaohua, and Chen Shangsheng. *History of China's Overseas Communications*. China Social Sciences Press, 2017.

Chen, Guoqiang, and Chen Qingfa. *Research on the Hui People in Baiqi*. Xiamen University Press, 1993.

Chen, Guoqiang. *Research on the History of the Hui People in Chendai*. China Social Sciences Press, 1991.

Chen, Jianzhong, and Chen Lihua. *Fujian Dehua Kilns*. Lingnan Fine Arts Publishing House, 2003.

Chen, Jianzhong, Chen Lihua, and Chen Lifang. *History of Dehua Porcelain of China*. Shanghai Jiaotong University Press, 2011.

Chen, Jianzhong. *Dehua Kilns*. Fujian Fine Arts Publishing House, 2005.

Chen, Jiarong. *History of Communications between China and Foreign Countries*. Hong Kong Xuejin Bookstore, 1987.

Chen, Pengpeng. *Quanzhou Cultural Relics Manual*. Compiled and printed by Quanzhou Cultural Relics Management Committee, 2000.

[Ming] Chen, Rang. *Shao Wu Fu Zhi*. Annotated by Yang Qide, Fu Huanmin, Ye Xiaofan. Publishing House of Local Records, 2004.

Chen, Shengming. *Ming Cheng Ji*. Xiamen University Press, 2015.

Chen, Sidong. *Xing Yuan Bi Geng Lu*. Lujiang Publishing House, 2003.

Chen, Yan. *The Maritime Silk Road and Cultural Exchange between China and Foreign Countries*. Peking University Press, 1996.

[Tang] Chen, Zangqi. *Supplements of Materia Medica*. Edited by Shang Zhijun. Research Office of Southern Anhui Medical College, 1983.

Chen, Ziqiang. *Ancient Overseas Communications and Marine Culture of Zhangzhou*. Fujian People's Publishing House, 2014.

Chendai Town Hui Affairs Committee. *Jinjiang City Museum Chendai Hui History Museum*. 2002.

China and Maritime Silk Road Research Center, et al. *The Maritime Silk Road Research 1: Maritime Silk Road and Islamic Culture*. Fujian Education Press, 1997.

———. *The Maritime Silk Road Research 2: China and Southeast Asia*. Fujian Education Press, 1999.

———. *The Maritime Silk Road Research 4: A Collection of Chen Dasheng's Research Papers on Islam and Arab Inscriptions*. Fujian Education Press, 2007.

China Institute of Navigation and Quanzhou Municipal People's Government. *Quanzhou Port and Maritime Silk Road*. China Social Sciences Press, 2002.

———. *The Quanzhou Port and the Maritime Silk Road 2*. China Social Sciences Press, 2003.

China Overseas Communication History Research Association and Quanzhou Maritime Museum. *Compilation of Quanzhou Overseas Historical Communications Materials*. Quanzhou Maritime Museum (internal handout), 1983.

Cui, Yong, Zhang Yongqiang, and Xiao Dashun. *Dunhuang at Sea: Nanhai Number One and Other Maritime Cultural Relics*. Guangdong Economic Press, 2015.

Dai, Xingzhen. "Food Culture Exchanges between China and Foreign Countries in the Yuan Dynasty." Master's thesis, Jinan University, 2007.

[Italian] D'Ancona, Jacob. *The City of Light*. Translated by [English] David Selburn, Yang Min, et al. Shanghai People's Publishing House, 1999.

[English] Donnelly, Ignatius Loyola. *Chinese White—Fujian Dehua Porcelain*. Translated by Wu Longqing. Fujian Fine Arts Publishing House, 2006.

[Tang] Duan, Chengshi. *The Miscellaneous Morsels from Youyang*. Zhonghua Book Company, 1981.

[Tang] Duan, Gonglu. *Bei Hu Lu (with notes)*. Annotated by Cui Guitu. Zhonghua Book Company, 1985.

Fang, Hao. *The History of Communication between China and the West*. Shanghai People's Publishing House, 2008.

Feng, Xiaoqi. *Research on Ancient Export Porcelain*. Forbidden City Publishing House, 2013.

[French] Ferrand, Gabriel. *Annotation to the Oriental Literature of the Persian Turks.* Translated by Geng Sheng and Mu Genlai. Zhonghua Book Company, 1989.

Fujian Museum and Jinjiang Museum. *The Cizao Kiln Site.* Science Press, 2011.

Fujian Provincial Chronicle Compilation Committee. *Historical Atlas of Fujian.* Fujian Provincial Map Publishing House, 2004.

Fujian Provincial Museum. *Dehua Kilns.* Cultural Relics Publishing House, 1990.

———. *The Zhangzhou Kiln: An Investigation and Excavation Report of Ming and Qing Dynasty Kiln Sites in Zhangzhou, Fujian.* Fujian People's Publishing House, 1997.

[Japanese] Fujita, Toyohachi. *Research on Ancient Traffic in the South China Sea.* Translated by He Jianmin. Shanxi People's Publishing House, 2015.

[Japanese] ———. *Song Bureau for Foreign Shipping and Its Regulations.* Translated by Wei Chongqing. Shanxi People's Publishing House, 2015.

[Ming] Gong, Zhen. *The Annals of Foreign Nations in the Western Ocean.* Annotated by Xiang Da. Zhonghua Book Company, 2012.

Guo, Moruo. *Historical Chinese Atlas.* China Cartographic Publishing House, 1996.

[Japanese] Hayashi, Kenzo. *Research on East Asian Musical Instruments.* Translated by Qian Daosun. Shanghai Bookstore Publishing House, 2013.

He, Chengfeng. *Yonglong Tongbao Qian Fan.* Zhonghua Book Company, 2005.

[Ming] He, Qiaoyuan. *Book of Min.* Collated by the Institute of Ancient Books, Department of History, Xiamen University. Fujian People's Publishing House, 1995.

[Ming] ———. *The Complete Works of Jingshan.* Sorted by Fujian Provincial Institute of Literature and History. Fujian People's Publishing House, 2015.

He, Zhenliang, and Lin Demin. *Cizao Ceramics.* Xiamen University Press, 2005.

He, Zhenliang, Lin Demin, and Pei Guanghui. *Cizao Kiln Porcelain.* Fujian Fine Arts Publishing House, 2002.

[Qing] Huai, Yinbu, ed. *Quanzhou Prefecture Chronicles.* Written by Huang Ren and Guo Gengwu (Qianlong). Shanghai Bookstore Publishing House, 2000.

Huang, Chunyan. *Overseas Trade in the Song Dynasty.* Social Sciences Academic Press (China), 2003.

[Ming] Huang, Shengzeng. *Records of Tributes from the West Seas.* Annotated by Xie Fang. Zhonghua Book Company, 2008.

Huang, Tianzhu. *Quanzhou Ji Gu Ji.* China Federation of Literary and Art Circles Press, 2003.

Huang, Zhongjie. "Research on Several Issues of Quanzhou Islamic Stone Carving Art." Master's thesis, Fujian Normal University, 2007.

[Japanese] Kuwabara, Jitsuzō. *Research on Trade Ports in the Tang and Song Dynasties.* Translated by Yang Lian. Shanxi People's Publishing House, 2015.

[Japanese] ———. *Stories of Pu Shougeng.* Translated by Chen Yujing. Zhonghua Book Company, 1954.

[American] Laufer, Berthold. *Sino-Iranica.* Translated by Lin Junyin. Commercial Press, 2015.

Lai, Shanshan. "The Marine Culture in the Lower River Min from the Shipwreck in Dinghai Bay." Master's thesis, Xiamen University, 2009.

Lai, Yuanqian. "Research on the Modular Systems of the Main Body Pattern of Clark Porcelain Plates." Master's thesis, Jingdezhen Ceramic University, 2014.

Leading Group for the Commemoration of the 600th Anniversary of Zheng He's Voyages to the West. *Sail across the Oceans—Commemorating the 600th Anniversary of Zheng He's Voyages to the West*. China Social Sciences Press, 2005.

[Southern Dynasties, Song Dynasty] Lei, Xiao. *Lei Gong Pao Zhi Lun*. supplemented by [Qing]Zhang Ji, and annotated by Shi Zhongan. Jiangsu Science and Technology Press, 1985.

Li, Donghua. *Quanzhou and China's Medieval Maritime Traffic*. Taiwan Student Book Company, 1986.

Li, Guangbin. *Study on Ibn Battuta's Journey to China*. Ocean Publishing House, 2009.

Li, Jiping, Zhu Xuequn, and Wang Lianmao. *Quanzhou Culture and Maritime Silk Road*. Social Sciences Academic Press, 2007.

Li, Qingxin. *The Maritime Silk Road*. China Intercontinental Press, 2006.

Li, Shaohua. "History of Import of Arabian Fragrance and Its Influence on Traditional Chinese Medicine." Master's thesis, Beijing University of Traditional Chinese Medicine, 2005.

Li, Xiaoxia. "Research on *Junchi* (kettle)." Master's thesis, Shandong University, 2013.

Li, Xiaoyun. "Research on Foreign Objects in the Song Dynasty." Master's thesis, Henan University, 2013.

Li, Xuan. "The Influence of Exotic Culture on Yuan and Ming blue-and-white Porcelain." Master's thesis, Jingdezhen Ceramic University, 2014.

Li, Yukun, and Li Xiumei. *History of Overseas Communications of Ancient Quanzhou*. China Radio and Television Press, 2006.

Li, Yukun. *A Brief History of Quanzhou Overseas Communications*. Xiamen University Press, 1995.

[Ming] Li, Guangjin. *Jing Bi Ji*. Checked by Zeng Xiangbo. Fujian People's Publishing House, 2012.

[Ming] Li, Shizhen. *Compendium of Materia Medica*. Chongwen Book Company, 2015.

[Five Dynasties] Li, Xun. *Sea Herbs and Materia Medica (annotated edition)*. Edited and annotated by Shang Zhijun. People's Medical Publishing House, 1997.

Liao, Dake. *Fujian Overseas Traffic History*. Fujian People's Publishing House, 2002.

Lin, Tianwei. *History of Fragrance Trade in the Song Dynasty*. Hong Kong Chinese Society, 1960.

Liu, Dongxue. "The Influence of Overseas Trade on the Development of Traditional Chinese Medicine in the Song Dynasty." Master's thesis, Shanghai Normal University, 2011.

[Tang] Liu, Xun et al. *Eight Kinds of Notes in Regions South of the Five Ridges in Past Dynasties*. Annotated by Lu Xun and Yang Weiqun. Guangdong People's Publishing House, 2011.

Liu, Yingsheng. *Talk about the Silk Road*. Anhui People's Publishing House, 2017.

Lü, Jin. "The Co-Prosperity of Chinese blue-and-white Porcelain Art and Islamic Decoration in the 13th to 15th Century." Master's thesis, Jingdezhen Ceramic University, 2014.

[Song] Lü, Yihao. *Zhong Mu Ji, Emperor's Four Treasuries No. 1131 Ji Bu 70 Collections*. Shanghai Ancient Books Publishing House, 1987.

Ma, Jian, trans. *The Koran*. China Social Sciences Press, 2011.

[Ancient Arabia] Masudi, Abu Hasan Ali b. Husayn b. Ali. *The Golden Prairie*. Translated by Geng Sheng. China Tibetology Press, 2013.

[Tang] Meng, Shen. *Dietary Materia Medica*. Supplemented by [Tang] Zhang Ding, annotated by Wu Shouju, Yu Jin. China Commercial Press, 1992.

[Ming] Miao, Xiyong. *Ben Cao Jing Shu*. Jiangsu Guangling Ancient Book Press, 1984.

[Japanese] Mikami, Tsukio. *The Road of Ceramics: An Exploration of Contact Points between Eastern and Western Civilizations*. Translated by Hu Defen. Tianjin People's Publishing House, 1983.

Nanjing County Committee of the Chinese People's Political Consultative Conference. *The Nanjing Dongxi Kiln and Foreign Trade in the Ming and Qing Dynasties*. Fujian People's Publishing House, 2016.

[Japanese] Ōba, Osamu, [American] V. A. Sogorov, [American] I. A. Donnelly, and [Japanese] Anonymous. *Textual Research on Tang Ship Painting· Chinese Ship· Chinese Wooden Sailboat*. Translated by Chen Jinghua and Zhu Jiajun, checked by Chen Yanhang, Wang Feng. Ocean Press, 2013.

[Song] Ouyang, Xiu. *The New History of the Five Dynasties*. Annotated by [Song] Xu Wudang. Zhonghua Book Company, 2016.

[Italian] Polo, Marco. *The Travels of Marco Polo*. Translated by Feng Chengjun. Shanghai Bookstore Publishing House, 1999.

[Ming] Qi, Jiguang. *New Treatise on Military Efficiency*. Annotated by Sheng Dongling. Zhonghua Book Company, 1996.

Quanzhou Harbor Group and Quanzhou Port Association. *The Quanzhou Port and Maritime Silk Road 3: A Collection of Essays to Commemorate the 600th Anniversary of Zheng He's Voyages to the West*. China Social Sciences Press, 2005.

Quanzhou History Research Association of Quanzhou City. *Selected Materials of Hui Family Genealogy in Quanzhou*, 1979.

Quanzhou Maritime Museum. *Excavation and Research of Ships in Song Dynasty in Quanzhou Bay*. Ocean Press, 1987.

Quanzhou Maritime Museum. *Proceedings of the Symposium on Maritime Communications and Islamic Culture*. Quanzhou Maritime Museum (internal handout), 2008.

———. *Survey Data of Quanzhou Overseas Communication History Vol. 5: Special Edition of Pu Shougeng's Family*.

Quanzhou Overseas Transportation History Museum, Quanzhou History Research Association. *Selected Papers on Islamic Studies in Quanzhou*. Fujian People's Publishing House, 1983.

[Italian] Romani, Francesca Romana. *Islam: The Light of Arab Civilization*. Translated by Sun Haipeng. Hebei Education Press, 2013.

[English] Royle, John Forbes. *A Manual of Materia Medica and Therapeutics*. Translated by [English] John Fryer, edited by [Qing] Zhao Yuanyi. Jiangnan Manufacturing Bureau of Qing Dynasty.

[American] Schafer, Edward Hetzel. *The Golden Peaches of Samarkand: A Study of Tang Exotics*." Translated by Wu Yugui. Social Sciences Literature Publishing House, 2016.

[Han] Sima, Qian. *The Records of the Grand Historian*. Compiled and annotated by [Song] Pei Yin, indexed by [Tang] Sima Zhen, and corrected by [Tang] Zhang Shoujie. Zhonghua Book Company, 2014.

[Song] Shen, Kuo. *The Dream Pool Essays*. Shanghai Bookstore Publishing House, 2003.

Song, Xian. *Hui Yao Fang Kao Shi*. Zhonghua Book Company, 2000.

State Administration of Cultural Heritage. *Maritime Silk Road*. Cultural Relics Press, 2014.

Su, Jilang. *Ci Tong Meng Hua Lu*. Translated by Li Runqiang. Zhejiang University Press, 2012.

Su, Peiquan. "Blue and White Porcelain and Cultural Exchange between China and Foreign Countries." Ph.D. dissertation, Jinan University, 2005.

[Song] Su, Song. *Illustrated Materia Medica (annotated edition)*. Annotated by Hu Naichang and Wang Zhipu. Fujian Science and Technology Press, 1988.

Sun, Lingzhi. "Research on the History of Fragrance in the Ming and Qing Dynasties." Ph.D. dissertation, China Academy of Chinese Medical Sciences, 2015.

Tan, Qixiang. *Atlas of Chinese History*. China Cartographic Publishing House, 1982.

[Song] Tang, Shenwei. *Zheng Lei Materia Medica*. Annotated by [Song] Cao Xiaozhong, interpreted by Kou Zongshi. Shanghai Ancient Books Publishing House, 1991.

[Song] Tao, Gu. *Qing Yi Lu*. Zhonghua Book Company, 1991.

[Ming] Teng, Hong. *Classic of the Materia Medica*. Edited by [Qing] Gu Guanguang. Hunan Science and Technology Press, 2008.

The Fujian Museum. *The Long Silk Road: Relics of the Maritime Silk Road*. Fujian Education Press, 2013.

The Maritime Silk Road Research Center. *Crossing the Ocean: Cultural Heritage Exhibition of the Eight Cities Along China's Maritime Silk Road*. Ningbo Publishing House, 2012.

Tian, Ruying. "As Expensive as Pepper: Spices and Social Life in Western Europe from the 14th to the 16th Centuries." Ph.D. dissertation, Capital Normal University, 2013.

[Yuan] Tuo, et al. *History of the Song Dynasty*. Zhonghua Book Company, 1985.

Wan, Shi. *Genealogy of the Guo Family in Baiqi*. Compiled and printed by the Revision Committee of the Genealogy of the Guo Family in Baiqi, 2000.

[Yuan] Wang, Dayuan, interpreted by Su Jiqing, *A Brief Account of Island Barbarians*, Zhonghua Book Company, 1981.

Wang, Hongtao. *Wan Can Ji*. Edited by Wang Sida. Huaxing Publishing House, 1993.

[Ming] Wang, Minghe, ed. *Deng Tan Bi Jiu*. Collected by Harvard-Yenching Library, Harvard University. Published during the reign of the Wanli Emperor in the Ming Dynasty.

[Song] Wang, Pu. *Institutional History of the Tang Dynasty*. Zhonghua Book Company, 2017.

Wang, Xibo. "Research on the Relationship between Ancient Chinese Export Porcelain and the Development of Southeast Asian Ceramics." Ph.D. dissertation, Yunnan University, 2015.

Wang, Xintian. "History of the Development of Maritime Porcelain Industry in Southeast China." Ph.D. dissertation, Xiamen University, 2007.

[Tang] Wei, Zheng, et al. *Book of Sui*. Zhonghua Book Company, 1973.

Wu, Jing. "Research on Ceramic Utensils in Persian Miniature Paintings." Master's thesis, Jingdezhen Ceramic Institute, 2012.

Wu, Juanjuan. "Spice and Social Life in the Tang Dynasty." Master's thesis, Anhui University, 2010.

Wu, Qisheng. *Zhangzhou Kilns in Ming and Qing Dynasties*. Fujian People's Publishing House, 2015.

Wu, Wenliang, and Wu Youxiong. *Religious Rock Carvings in Quanzhou (updated edition)*. Science Press, 2005.

[Song] Wu, Zimu. *Meng Liang Lu*. Commercial Press, 1939.

Xia, Shihua. "Economic Research on Fragrance Industry in Song Dynasty." Ph.D. dissertation, Shaanxi Normal University, 2012.

———. "Investigation on the Phenomenon of Fragrance in the Song Dynasty." Master's thesis, Jiangxi Normal University, 2003.

Xu, Hui. *Plants on the Silk Road*. Qingdao Publishing House, 2016.

———. *Spices on the Silk Road*. Qingdao Publishing House, 2016.

[Qing] Xu, Song. *Supplementary Notes on the Biography of the Western Regions of the Book of Han*. Zhonghua Book Company, 1985.

Xu, Tingting. "The Spread and Influence of Chinese Ceramic Culture in Southeast Asia from the 11th to the 19th Century." Master's thesis, Jingdezhen Ceramic University, 2013.

Xu, Yuanyuan. "Research on the Import of South China Sea Fragrance and Its Medical Value in the Tang Dynasty." Master's thesis, Shaanxi Normal University, 2015.

Xu, Yunqiao. *Annotations of Xu Zhong's Southern Grasses*. Institute of Southeast Asian Studies, 1970.

[Tang] Xuanzang, and Bianji. *Annotations on The Great Tang Records on the Western Regions*. Annotated by Ji Xianlin. Zhonghua Book Company, 2000.

[Ming] Yan, Congjian. *Shu Yu Zhou Zi Lu*. Edited by Yu Sili. Zhonghua Book Company, 2009.

Yan, Xiaoqing. "Research on the Production, Utilization, and Trade of Plant Spices in Ancient China." Ph.D. dissertation, Nanjing Agricultural University, 2008.

Yang, Enpu. *Maritime Silk Road: Embrace of Beginning and End*. Quanzhou Huaguang College (internal handout), 2015.

[Ming] Yang, Siqian. (Wanli) *Quanzhou Prefecture Chronicles*. Written by Huang Fengxiang et al. Taiwan Student Book Company, 1987.

Ye, Wencheng, and Lin Zhonggan. *Fujian Ceramics*. Fujian People's Publishing House, 1993.

Ye, Wencheng, and Wu Qisheng. *Ancient Chinese Ceramic Specimens: Fujian Zhang Kiln*. Lingnan Fine Arts Publishing House, 2002.

[Ming] Yu, Dayou. *Zheng Qi Tang Quan Ji*. Annotated by Liao Yuanquan and Zhang Jichang. Fujian People's Publishing House, 2007.

[Han] Yuan, Kang, and Wu Ping. *Yue Jue Shu*. Zhejiang Ancient Books Publishing House, 2013.

Zeng, Fan. *An Introduction to Fujian Ceramic Archaeology*. Fujian Map Publishing House, 2001.

[Jin] Zhang, Hua. *Records of Diverse Matters*. Zhonghua Book Company, 1985.

[Qing] Zhang, Lu. *Ben Jing Feng Yuan*. China Traditional Chinese Medicine Publishing House, 2007.

[Ming] Zhang, Xie. *Research on Eastern and Western Oceans*. Annotated by Xie Fang. Zhonghua Book Company, 2008.

[Han] Zhang, Zhongjing. *Essential Prescriptions from the Golden Cabinet*. Xueyuan Press, 2014.

Zhangzhou Political Consultative Conference Culture, Education, Health and Sports Committee. *Selected Papers on Zhangzhou's Maritime Silk Road*. Fujian People's Publishing House, 2016.

[Song] Zhao, Rushi. *A Description of Barbarian Nations, Records of Foreign People*. Annotated by Yang Bowen. Zhonghua Book Company, 2000.

Zhao, Wanying. "Research on the Development of Diet Therapy in Ancient China." Master's thesis, Northwest Agricultural University of Science and Technology, 2008.

Zheng, Xiaojun. "Ceramic Industry and Early Shipping Around the Kowloon River Estuary in Song and Yuan Dynasties." Master's thesis, Xiamen University, 2007.

[Yuan] Zhou, Daguan. *Annotations of The Customs of Cambodia*. Annotated by Xia Nai. Zhonghua Book Company, 1981.

[Song] Zhou, Mi. *Kui Xin Za Shi*. Annotated by Wu Qiming. Zhonghua Book Company, 1988.

[Song] Zhou, Qufei. *Annotation of Representative Answers from the Region beyond the Mountains*. Annotated by Yang Wuquan. Zhonghua Book Company, 1999.

Zhu, Jianqiu, and Li Wanquan. *Newly Organized Zheng He's Navigation Atlas*. People's Communications Publishing House, 1988.

[Song] Zhu, Yu. *Ping Zhou Ke Tan*. Annotated by Li Weiguo. Zhonghua Book Company, 2007.

Zhuang, Jinghui. *Ding's Ancestral Hall in Chendai*. Xiamen University Press, 2003.

———. *Genealogy of the Ding Family in Chendai*. Green Leaf Education Press, 1996.

———. *Research on Overseas Communication Footprints*. Xiamen University Press, 1996.

———. *Research on Quanzhou Port Archaeology and Overseas Communication History*. Yuelu Publishing House, 2006.

Zhuang, Weiji, Zhuang Jinghui, and Wang Lianmao. *The Famous Port of the Maritime Silk Road: Quanzhou*. Ocean Press, 1989.

Zhuang, Weiji. *Hai Shang Ji*. Xiamen University Press, 1996.

About the Chief Editor

Mr. Xie Bizhen, Professor and Doctoral Supervisor of Fujian Normal University, Director of the Fujian-Taiwan Regional Research Center of Fujian Normal University, a key research base of humanities and social sciences of the Ministry of Education. His main research focuses on Chinese overseas transportation and trade history, the history of Sino-Japanese relations, and the local history of Fujian.

About the Authors

Ding Yuling is an anthropologist and the director of the Quanzhou Maritime Museum in China's Fujian Province. She is also the executive vice president of the Chinese Society for the Study of Overseas Chinese and Maritime History.

Lin Han is a historian and curator at the Quanzhou Maritime Museum. His research interests include maritime and ship history. Both authors have participated in multiple research projects and have published academic papers and books in their respective fields.